MYSTIC Mothers

KEVIN ERNEST HALL

Introduction into
12 mystical women
from the Monastic Era

Published by Seraph Creative

Mystic Mothers
Copyright© 2020 by Kevin Ernest Hall

Published by Seraph Creative in 2020
United States / United Kingdom / South Africa / Australia
www.seraphcreative.org

Typesetting & Layout by Feline
www.felinegraphics.com

Printed in USA, UK and RSA, 2020

ISBN 978-0-6486986-5-4

I dedicate Mystic Mothers to Dr Adonijah Ogbonnaya,
as a mentor and spiritual father. His advice, guidance, and
theological understanding has shaped my understanding and
experience of all things spiritual. I have been learning from
this Spiritual giant since 2013.

Thank you Papa for all your sacrifice, hard work and hours of
patience with your son.

Foreword

Kevin Hall is one of most genuine and teachable people I've met. Kevin loves the Lord with a passion and intensity that is simply beautiful. His heart of love is carried into the writing of this beautiful book. You can sense the tenderness and sincere care on ever page. It is an unexpected surprise to see such a rich collection of Saints in one volume and I'm thrilled to see this book released. Kevin brings into clear focus the hidden mystical mothers of church history. Drawing out ancient wisdom making it fresh and relevant for now. I valued the addition of his own personal contemplative experiences with the Saints into the chapters. It is provocative and makes me hungry for my own unique encounters. This book is timely, nourishing and hope filled. I highly commend this book to you and hope it expands your heart and takes you deeper still into your mystical union with God.

Justin Paul Abraham
Company of Burning Hearts

Acknowledgements

Thank you Jesus for giving me the grace to write this book, I appreciate Holy Spirit; you have poured into my life to learn all your ways. To Chris Blackeby and the publishing team, thank you for all the hours of editing, and hard work behind the scenes. To Joseph Sturgeon and his wife, thank you for all your support and encouragement in this process.

To Justin Abraham, thank you for being a true friend, and an older brother in the Lord, your life has changed me deeply.

To my parents and friends all over the world, thank you for standing with me during all the hard times, and the fun moments, I appreciate all the colors life has brought to help me paint pictures with my words.

Thank you to Nathan and Ryan my sons, for teaching your Dad so much, you have changed me in every way possible, I love being your dad.

Introduction

When the topic of one's book is 12 female mystics that changed the world, one realizes that this is probably a task best reserved for the women of our Christian faith.

However, I felt so inspired by the lives of these women, and their search for God, that I felt it necessary to capture some of their treasures in this book.

The first question I think many asks is why these 12 mystics, and my answer is very simple: personal resonance and prayer. I choose these mystics based on their path, and how my life interjected with theirs without planning or prior forethought. How their journeys resonated with my personal journey as a seeker of truth and a recipient of divine grace.

The aim of this book is not to write an academic work, or an exhaustive explanation of their theology. The focus will be a synopsis of their lives, their work, and some personal revelation I have received by engaging with them at various times in my life and in the many different ways I was affected.

Coming from a protestant and charismatic background, I have found some of their theology and their ideas to be different than my own, I however chose to delve deeper into their revelations of Jesus, and focus less on some of their ideas that were more at home with the time and place of their lives. Our milieu sometimes has a bigger effect on our theology than we expect, so with a gracious and forgiving intent, read about their experiences of the divine, and gloss over their more medieval ideas.

As with most Christian traditions, many works on their theology and their lives have been written, trying to explain, or in some way understand what they describe in their writings. I did not choose a neat chronical order, or any other form of alphabetical arrangement, these women deserve their own appraisal without the need to complicate the book with too many details and context which might cloud the readers perspective, read them as they are written, encounter them as they deserve, here and now, let their voices speak to you as your read about their lives.

I would like to address some doctrinal concerns some might have when reading the mystics and trying to understand their language. My protestant friends have great objections to some of the ideas of the mystics, and in some cases I might agree. Let's be honest, we all have many disagreements about these practices, the aim of this book is not to discuss Catholic and Protestant doctrine, there is ample scholarly work done on these differences.

I would encourage the reader to consider this, all denominations in Christianity who confess Jesus as Lord and believes in the Trinity are all Christian in their nature, our differences are not greater than our agreements, and we need to focus on Christ as the center point.

When I paint with the brush of doctrine, I choose to do so graciously, and mercifully, choosing to give all sides the benefit of the doubt. I am not Catholic, but in saying so, I do have some sympathetic views on their ideas.

One of the most offensive ideas in this book will be the thought of mysticism today, our ability to encounter and have a relationship with the saints, I realize this is exotic theology to some, and just plain blasphemy or heresy to others, I would encourage you to simply read the lives of the saints, and examine their lessons.

As I write this, our current society is saturated with the supernatural, the mystical, the un-explainable, like never before in history.

We have become disillusioned with our materialistic world view, and our scientific discoveries are starting to explain for the first time some dimensional and multi-dimensional quantum realities, and as students of the spiritual world, we come full circle to search for something deeper than our natural instrument and current abilities predict.

> *"Those who cannot **remember** the past are **condemned to repeat** it"* - George Santayana

Why do I believe the mystics have some relevance to our society? Well, understanding our development in context always helps to grow our appreciation for the giants who have walked in the path we now easily traverse, because of their pioneering work.

Or as the Methodist Theologian **Albert C. Outler** wrote as the 4 sources of theological development:

- Scripture
- Tradition
- Reason
- Christian Experience

We want to explore the mystics as both the Tradition and Christian Experience, some mystics would fit both of these disciplines / ideas, like Terresa of Avila – a Doctor of the church. However we classify them, the rich history of the church needs to be firmly in our hearts and minds as we seek to experience the divine reality of God in our daily lives.

While writing this book, I had a dream; in the dream I am gazing at the beautiful glass work in the cathedrals, and looking to find God in the church I was in. I looked everywhere, I stood at the statues of the saints, I gazed at the beauty of the cross depicted in the cathedral, but I felt no sense of God.

As I walked out of the cathedral, I saw a young child begging, and slowly walked up to him, something about him was strange. I gave him some food, and change I had in my pocket, while looking into his eyes, they turned dark blue, and then the small child spoke, in the voice of Jesus: "My son, find me in the eyes of the poor, and you will find me everywhere you go in life".

I realized with this dream that when we read the mystics, and their desire for poverty, we often judge their actions, however the "Poor in Spirit" is quoted in the words of Christ, maybe some of their desire was to mimic Jesus, and be found where He is often most welcome, in the hearts and minds of the poor and broken.

I trust you are able to use the thoughts in this book to spur you onwards and upwards in your journey towards knowing Jesus, my one desire is to see Him grow in the corners of your heart, into a garden of intimacy and joy.

May these mystics, these honorable women, ignite your passion anew for the Christ, Jesus, our Lord.

INDEX

Background of the Medieval Times

Before we start on our journey of discovering the ideas and lives of these remarkable women, lets first look at the time in which they lived, and the context in history.

The feudal system of Europe was entrenched for hundreds of years, and people were focused on the land, the season and the progression of nature, this provided a level of certainty and predictability in their lives. Feudalism gave way to the Renaissance, as urbanization started in Europe.

The people living in cities were presented with their own challenges and thoughts, and thus created places where ideas were share more frequently. The change also created uncertainty and an explosion of thought and invention.

Women however still had very little say in this society, their voices muffled by the system, focused on production and productivity. In the faith community, they had relatively little input, the legitimacy of their thoughts and ideas had to be transmitted by men in their congregation or thought leaders in the ecclesiastical world, credibility was won not on the basis of achieving but rather steeped in the traditions of men.

In many cases the women found male confessors to help them in their path towards cultural impact.

The church was also in the process of reform, the order of the catholic church was changing, giving more opportunities to some, and providing the ability for lay ministers and women to become part of the faithful without the need to become nuns, monks or priests.

Other orders like the Carmelite nuns, the Benedictines and the Franciscans had a great focus on the poor and needy, allowing them to focus and provide care for the destitute in society

The response by the church to the urban needs of the population created the need for these orders to provide pastoral care and compassion to the congregants, and those attending services and cathedrals.

When reading the lives of the mystics, they were not placed in the easy times in history, their lives, like light beacons in the annals of time, seem to remind us that we shine at our brightest when the world is at its darkest.

The escape from the dark ages are in part due to the light of Christ shining through the lives of these mystics, these misfits, these bunch of women who chose the path lest traveled, to help humanity through this phase of development.

Many of these women lived in the time of the black plague that peaked between 1347 and 1351, killing between 70 to 200 million people in Europe.

The effect of this plague on the physiological development of Europe was huge, and the tremendous trauma experienced by society, some estimate almost a third of Europe was wiped out by this sickness.

Timeline

Bridget of Ireland	451 - 525
Hilda of Whitby	614 - 680
Hildegard of Bingen	1098 - 1179
Mechthild of Magdeburg	1207 - 1282/94
Gertrude the Great	1256 - 1302
Julian of Norwich	1342 - 1416
Catherine of Sienna	1347 - 1380
Bridget of Sweden	1303 - 1373
Catherine of Genoa	1447 - 1510
Teresa of Avila	1515 - 1582
Jeanne Guyon	1648 - 1717
Therese of Lisieux	1873 - 1897

CHAPTER 1
Julian of Norwich

"The Love of God is hard and marvelous. It cannot and will not be broken because of our sins"

Julian of Norwich

Born:	1342
Died:	1416
Nationality:	England
Location:	Norwich
Outlook:	Ancorite
Books:	Revelations of Divine Love (1410)
	Short Texts (1373)
Interests:	Theologian, Spiritual writer, Mystic
Achievements:	She wrote the earliest surviving book in the English language to be written by a woman.
Key Teachings:	The Motherhood of God – Jesus, The passion of Christ
	All is well and all shall be well". She believed in the mystery that all would be well (restoration of all things).

The Life of Julian (Vita)

Very few details remain of Julian's early life. For one, we are not sure what her actual name is. What is known is that she was born in Norfolk in 1342 and that she stayed in Norwich. Norwich had a church by the name of St Julian. This is the church where she spent most of her life in a cell attached to the church.

She was educated at Carrow Abbey, by Benedictine nuns, this was a well-known place of education for young ladies at the time. At the age of 30, she started to receive visions from God, on what she then believed to be her deathbed. These visions later became the texts for her work, "Reflections of divine love".

She wrote two versions of her visions; the "short text", which is just the visions she received of Jesus and the "long text", which is her own theological exploration of what these visions might mean. The long text was finished in 1410, almost 30 years after the experiences started.

Julian preferred solitude and silence. She lived in what is known as an anchorite cell, attached to the church. An anchorite cell is a small room that is built against the church wall. This services to isolate and give the anchorite the ability to retract from normal life and only focus on God. Although Julian lived in this manner, the community still came to her cell for advice and she was known for her wisdom and insight.

In 1414, when she was 70, she was visited by an English mystic, Margery Kempe, who mentioned Julian in her book; "The Book of Margery Kempe".

Julian died at the age of 74 in Norwich, and a shrine has been set up for her at the St Julian's church in Norwich.

Theology of Julian of Norwich

"A Theology of Compassion"

Julian's major focus was the "problem of sin". In her work she focuses on human nature, the original sin, and how we work towards the resolution of our depravity.

Many mystics have this focus, but few found the answers that Julian had found, in the way she found them. How did she find the answers to life's most enduring questions?

As Julian gazes into the suffering of Jesus, she sees the suffering of her own life, Jesus seeing the intimacy of His suffering being revealed to her.

Revelations of Divine Love – Page 85 of The Elevated Joys of Christ

And Christ rejoices that He is our Brother, and Jesus rejoices that He is our Savior. These are five high joys, as I understand, in which He wills that we enjoy: Him praising, Him thanking, Him loving, Him endlessly blessing.

Revelations of Divine Love – Page 90

Highly aught we to rejoice that God dwells in our soul, and much more highly aught we to rejoice that our soul dwells in God. Our soul is made to be God's dwelling-place; and the dwelling-place of the soul is God, which is unmade. And high understanding it is, inwardly to see and know that God, which is our Maker, dwells in our soul; and an higher understanding it is, inwardly to see and to know that our soul, that is made, dwells in God's Substance: of which Substance, God, we are that we are.

Revelations of Divine Love – Page 93

God is nearer to us than our own Soul: for He is the Ground in whom our Soul stands, and He is the Mean that keeps the Substance and the Sense-nature together so that they shall never be separated. For our soul sits in God in very rest, and our soul stands in God in very strength, and our Soul is kindly rooted in God in endless love: and for that if we will have knowledge of our Soul, and communing and dalliance with it, it is fitting for to seek to our Lord God in whom it is enclosed. (And of this enclosement I saw and understood more in the Sixteenth Shewing, as I shall tell.)

Revelation of Divine Love – Page 100

Jesus our Very Mother in Nature by virtue of our first making; and He is our Very Mother in Grace, by taking our nature made. All the fair working, and all the sweet natural office of precious Motherhood is allocated to the Second Person: for in Him we have this Godly Will whole and safe without end, both in Nature and in Grace, of His own proper Goodness. I understood three manners of seeing of Motherhood in God: the first is grounded in our

Nature's making; the second is taking of our nature, - and there begins the Motherhood of Grace; the third is Motherhood of working, - and in it is a distribution by the same Grace, of length and breadth and height and of deepness without end. And all is one Love.

Revelation of Divine Love – Page 102

He might no more die, but He would not stint of working: wherefore then it is fitting for Him to feed us; for the precious love of Motherhood has made Him debtor to us. The mother may give her child suck of her milk, but our precious Mother, Jesus, He may feed us with Himself, and does it, courteously and tenderly, with the Blessed Sacrament that is precious food of my life; and with all the sweet Sacraments He sustains us mercifully and graciously

Revelation of Divine Love – Page 102

He will have all our love fastened to Him. And in this I saw that all our duty that we owe, by God's bidding, to Fatherhood and Motherhood, for reason of God's Fatherhood and Motherhood is fulfilled in true loving of God, which blessed love Christ works in us. And this was shewed in all the Revelations and especially in the high plenteous words where He says: It is I that you love.

Revelations of Divine Love – Page 134

The properties are these: Life, Love, and Light.

In life is marvelous homeliness, and in love is gentle courtesy, and in light is endless Nature-hood. These properties were in one Goodness: to which Goodness my Reason would be joined and cleave to it with all its might. I saw with reverent fear, and highly marveling in the sight and in the feeling of the sweet accord, that our Reason is in God; understanding that it is the highest gift that we have received; and it is grounded in nature. Our faith is a light by nature coming of our endless Day, that is our Father, God. In which light our Mother, Christ, and our good Lord, the Holy Spirit, leads us in this passing life. This light is measured discreetly, need fully standing to us in the night

Personal Journey with Julian of Norwich

I was invited to speak at a conference in the UK in 2017, this is when I was engaged by Julian of Norwich as I was reading about all of the amazing saints there had been in the UK over the years.

She shared with me the understanding of God as both male and female, and

God not having any sexuality but more an understanding of the feminine energetic system. This was mostly a foreign concept to me, but I loved the way it explained Galatians 3:28: "There is neither Jew nor Gentile, neither slave nor free, nor is there male and female, for you are all one in Christ Jesus."

One day as I was meditating, Julian rushed into the room, almost like a child skipping on a sea of grass. I looked at her sense of joy, complete bliss and wonderment were part of her being, radiating pure passion, pure joy.

It was so refreshing just to speak to Julian as some of the other mystics were more careful in their words, more measured in their manner and she seemed to drink up the moments of life, and the time with God, like a thirsty desert dweller, her gulps of enjoyment made me wonder about our ability to enjoy this life of Abundance, Jesus Christ promised us.

Julian explained the wonder of life, the need to enjoy the goodness of God in the midst of difficult life circumstances. She admonished me to experience Christ more deeply until the rich pearls of His love, would diminish the cares of this world, and pride of life, and it's other commitments.

Julian loves the nurturing aspect of God's love, not just the creator with power, but the creator which longs for His creation to experience the gambit of creation, without the need to overburden the creation.

This nurturing aspect brough Julian to the Sacred Feminine of the Trinity. We need to start from the onset to say, God is neither Male nor Female, but the feminine and male energy is inherent in the Divine being.

When God said let "us" create man in our image, he created Adam in a singular capacity, where male and female were in one person. When God removed the female from Adam, we understand that this feminine aspect of God, which was in Adam, was removed into a separate being, called Eve. In the same way, the Trinity of God, is constantly in complete union, and in perfect unity, not needing this division of being, since being God, the trinity is able to function outside of creation, with its intrinsic limitations.

God has many times been explained as a Father, but few times described as a Mother; the feminine aspect of nurture, care and comfort. The bible describes the Holy Spirit as Comforter; however, this is the same for the whole Trinity. When we experience God as Mother in all ways, when we understand the creative comfort that God brings to the conversation, we understand that there is no separation in God, and we start moving towards a concept of one-ness.

Sacred Feminine is described as the part of God that carries the feminine energetic system, this has less focus on feminine as a biological aspect, and more based on the nurturing capacity of God. If Adam was created male and female in God's image, the removal of Eve out of Adam, then means Eve is also part of God's divine image, hence the feminine aspect is present in God. This relates to the name of God El Shaddai -"the many breasted God" a clear metaphoric description of the nurturing sacred feminine.

Through the nurturing and comfort of the Sacred Feminine, we are confronted with rest. When you think about the traditional role of a father, without taking offence in the explanation, a father is the adventure and activity in the child's life. Whereas the mother brings the calm and rest and comfort to the child. Thus, through the engagement of the Sacred Feminine we are inherently engaging rest. Now then, from the other side we can also say that you can access the Sacred Feminine of the Trinity through rest. The aspects that will be found in the Sacred Feminine is mercy, celebration, beauty and maturing love.

The Sacred Feminine calls us also into a place of maturing love. Julian spoke at length about the process of maturing love that we as children of God need to cultivate for us to fully come to a place of one-ness.

The process of maturing love involves the following:

- Objectification of love

- Love of God based on our expectations

- Unconditional love of God

- Unconditional love for God

Job went through this process of maturing love when he lost everything. From a place of looking at the objects of our love as the motivator of the emotion to separating the love that we have towards the object to feel love without the object motivating the love.

His expectation of what he assumed God had to do to prove His love for him. So many times, our expectations of the love we want to receive from God is from a place of distrust and hurt. We need to learn to receive the love of God for what it is and not through our expectation thereof.

We must learn to accept the unconditional love of God. A love that will not be dictated to on who to love, for the word clearly speaks of God loving all his children without measure.

And lastly, we need to learn how to love God unconditionally. We need to create space within ourselves to love God without condition, where He can then start to manifest in us the abundant goodness that He has stored up for those that love Him.

QUESTIONS

1. What part of her life, and her challenges resonate with you ?

2. Which of the extract of Julian of Norwich's writing did you enjoy the most, and why did you enjoy that extract of "Revelation of Divine Love"?

3. What are your ideas of Love, and how would you describe love?

4. Do you think God loves you, and why?

5. If God loves you, what does unconditional love look like?

CHAPTER 2

Saint Hilda of Whitby

Prayer of Saint Hilda

May I be equal to Your hope of me.
If I am weak,
I ask that You send only what I can bear.
If I am strong,
may I shrink from no testing
that shall yield increase of strength
or win security for my spirit.
I trust in Thee, O Lord.
I say, ' Thou art my God.'
My times are in Thy hand,
my times are in Thy hand.

Born:	614
Died:	680
Nationality:	English
Location:	Whitby
Outlook:	Catholic and Celtic
Interests:	Mystic, writer, abbess
Achievements:	Synod of Whitby
Key Teachings:	Reconciliation
Supernatural Miracles:	Turning snakes into stones

The Life of Saint Hilda of Whitby

Hilda was born in 614 to a royal household in Deiran. While still a toddler, her father was poisoned at the royal court in current west Yorkshire.

Hilda grew up in King Edwin's court, where here adopted mother was the second wife of King Edwin, Bertha of Kent. She was a devout Roman Catholic and with her chaplain Paulinus of York, they influenced the royal court with their Augustinian ideas.

On 12 April 627 the whole court was baptized, including 13 year old Hilda, near York Minster. At the age of 33 Hilda moved from Chelles Abbey, to Northumbria, to become a nun, this was the request of Bishop Aidan of Lindisfarne.

Her first monastery was on the north bank of the River Wear, she practiced Celtic monasticism, which Bishop Aidan imported from Iona. After a year she was appointed as the second Abbess of Hartlepool Abbey.

In 657 Hilda was appointed the founding abbess of Whitby Abbey, where she remained until her death.

Hilda was known as an energetic, skilled teacher and administrator. She owned the land on which the monasteries were built and created flourishing communities where the focus was on farming, and famous for sheep, cattle and woodcutting.

Both the monasteries she led were arranged in the Celtic tradition, where men and women stayed separately in smaller houses of 2-4 people but worshiped together in the church.

She was known by the community for her divine wisdom and understanding in complex situations, which led to Princes and Royals seeking her out. She also had great care for the poor of the community and was considered a great leader.

The King Oswy chose her abbey to host the Synod of Whitby, the church needed to decide if they would follow Rome or the way of Iona, specifically the calculation of Easter. The Synod also had many other political and ecclesial issues, which ultimately led to the schism between the church of Northumbria and the church of Ireland.

This resulted in the Irish Celtic bishops retreating to Lindisfarne and later Iona. Hilda tirelessly worked to find common ground between the two sides, although her efforts might have failed, she felt great sadness for the division of the different Christian sects in England.

Ideas of Saint Hilda

Very little is written by Saint Hilda herself, so instead of writing her visions or experiences, I felt it would be more prudent to include some of what others write about her.

Most of her doctrine, theology and way of life, can be found in the Celtic mystic tradition of unity in diversity, and a love for the poor and needy in society.

Celtic theology is expressed in union, the idea that everything is connected, and that man is connected to nature and that our actions towards nature show our relationship with the divine. The earthy tones of this Celtic way of life did not sit well with the more austere faith of the rest of England, which at the time was focused on political power, and the royal courts.

As Bede writes in his Hagiography of Hilda

"Thus this servant of Christ, Abbess Hilda, whom all that knew her called Mother, for her singular piety and grace, was not only an example of good life, to those that lived in her monastery, but afforded occasion of amendment and salvation to many who lived at a distance, to whom the fame was brought of her industry and virtue; for it was necessary that the dream which her mother had, during her infancy, should be fulfilled".

My experience with Saint Hilda

My interest in this saint started with a uniquely personal journey, in 2017 I visited the UK for the first time, and on my journey chose to visit our family home in Staithes, a small fishing town on the coast of Yorkshire.

Whitby is one of the largest towns in the area, and the location of our great-grandmothers birth, when entering Whitby, the monastery ruins still has an allure and many family stories related to us. This place had great personal memories of my grandparents, and now as I walked into the ruins and prayed, I met with Hilda for the first time.

Hilda told of her heart broken feelings for the Celtic tradition that was lost, she explained that in some way, that day, the church rejected the mystics, the strange path of the Celtics, and Iona, for Rome, a more formal and well calculated learned way.

She told me how our current mystics were once again repeating the same mistakes of the past, how the move of the Holy Spirit had started to wane as the church was once again being rejected by the mystics this time.

The great reversal had taken place in our age, this time, the mystics birthed by the church, left the church, offended by her actions, her traditions, and her rules, they decided that God was no longer involved in the church, and their way, the higher way, the only way, and the better way.

During the next two years I experienced great suffering and personal hardship. I literally lost everything I held dear, yet as I look back on meeting Hilda, I realized, the joy set before me, just like with Jesus, was a church united in her love for Jesus, knowing that we are one body, one church, in heaven united to earth, all Christians everywhere, knowing we are growing to become more mature in this knowledge.

Shortly after this time, Hilda started speaking to me about the pathway I chose, I saw the wisdom of the mystics, living in communities, impacting their societies, not trying to create sub cultures of mystic ideas, but divinely becoming salt and light to the church, and the world.

This new journey was infinitely harder, yet profoundly deeper, more real, and impacted us on a historical level, I am not sure what God has planned for humanity, however I know this, mystics teach us that Jesus wants to speak, right now, right where you are reading these words, He is standing there, watching you, and wants you to know, He loves you more than you expect, dream or hope.

QUESTIONS

1. What part of her life, and her challenges resonate with you ?

2. IF we consider that her life story is really about reconciliation between different viewpoints, what do you think was the greatest obstacles she had ?

3. Is there people in your life God might want you to reconcile with ?

4. If reconciliation means finding common ground, what does this mean for your broken relationships?

5. Part of reconciliation is restitution, what would that mean to you in your relationships?

CHAPTER 3
Therese of Lisieux

"Jesus your arms are the elevator which lift me to heaven"

St Thérèse of Lisieux

Born:	1873
Died:	1897
Nationality:	France
Location:	Lisieux / Normandy
Outlook:	Carmelite Nun
Spiritual Director:	Jesuit, Father Pichon
Books:	The Story of a Soul
Interests:	Writing, Theology
Achievements:	Doctor of the Church
Key Teachings:	Simplicity, Constant kind acts, Care for the poor
Beatified:	29 April 1923
Canonized:	17 May 1925

The Life of Thérèse of Lisieux

Thérèse of Lisieux is the most modern of the saints covered in this book, and hence, there is more information available about this saint than most, her life has been well documented.

Although we only highlight some of the major events of her life, a more detailed and lengthy description can be found in her own writings. Well worth the read.

Thérèse was born on the 2nd of January 1873 in Alencon France, her father was a jeweler and her mother a successful lace-maker. So successful that her father ended up closing his watchmaking shop to work with her mother in the business of lacemaking. They had 9 children of which only 5 daughters survived; all of them become nuns.

Initially Thérèse was given to a wet nurse but at the age of 15 months she returned home to grow up with her family. She was brought up in a strict catholic house, her family practiced all the fasts, and disciplines of the catholic faith, visiting the poor and inviting vagabonds to their dinner table.

Her mother died on 28 August 1877, when she was 5 years old. This left a scar on her personality, and the joy she was known for disappeared to make way for a very scared, over-sensitive child.

Her father moved to Lisieux to be closer to his family, needing help with the 5 girls left in his care.

She went to school at the age of 8 at the Abbey of Notre Dame du Pre in Lisieux run by Benedictine nuns. The school was hard for her as she was bullied due to her good marks and would thus stay at home with her father.

Pauline, her older sister and confidant, left for the Carmelite convent at Lisieux in 1882, this setback had huge psychological effects on her. The trauma caused her to tremor and doctors saw this as a neurotic result due to the emotional distress. She was also diagnosed with scruples, a type of religious OCD disorder.

In 1886 she was converted at Christmas with an experience of Jesus at the local midnight mass. This conversion helped her overcome her sensitivity.

In 1887 her father took the family to Rome on a pilgrimage to the Vatican, she met the Pope Leo, and asked him to allow her to join the convent, at her young age of 15, the Pope responded that her superiors know best. She was dragged out of the Vatican halls, not wanting to leave the Pope's side.

On 18 April 1888 she joined the Carmelite convent in Lisieux, the same place where both her sisters were serving nuns. She took the habit on January 10, 1889 and focused on her studies of well-known mystics like John of the Cross.

In 1890 she completed her vows in the public ceremony, under the tutelage of Mother Marie de Gonzague. Her service to the church was focused on doing small acts of kindness and finding the divine in the mundane acts of life. She would seek out nuns in the convent who nobody would serve, and then endeavour to spend as much time with them as possible. In 1893 she was asked to be the assistant to the Novice mistress and help with the training of the novice nuns.

In 1896 she was diagnosed with Tuberculosis and spent the rest of the year completing her works, in anticipation of her death.

She died on 30 September 1897 aged 24, after having suffered much pain in the process, her doctors could not believe the amount of pain she endured without complaint.

Her last words were, *"My God, I love you!"*.

The Doctrine of Thérèse of Lisieux

Her doctrine is focused, as her name suggests, on the Face of Jesus.

Some of her teaching was based on the "little way": a lifestyle based on the ability to do works of service and focus on those around you without the need to focus on self.

St Thérèse of Lisieux Autobiography – Page 10

I am now at a time of life when I can look back on the past, for my soul has been refined in the crucible of interior and exterior trials. Now, like a flower after the storm, I can raise my head and see that the words of the Psalm are realized in me: "The Lord is my Shepherd and J shall want nothing. He has set me in a place of pasture. He has brought me up on the water of refreshment. He has converted my soul. He has led me on the paths of justice for His own Name's sake. For though I should walk in the midst of the shadow of death, I will fear no evils for Thou art with me." (cf. Psalms 23).

St Thérèse of Lisieux Autobiography – Page 29

Our Lord made me understand that the only true glory is that which lasts forever; and that to attain it there is no necessity to do brilliant deeds, but rather to hide from the eves of others, and even from oneself, so that "the left hand knows not what the right hand does." (cf. Mt 6:3). Then, as I reflected that I was born for great things, and sought the means to attain them, it was made known to me interiorly that my personal glory would never reveal itself before the eyes of men, but that it would consist in becoming a Saint.

St Thérèse of Lisieux Autobiography – Page 42

In this way He deigned to manifest Himself to our hearts; but how slight and transparent was the veil! Doubt was no longer possible; already Faith and Hope had given place to Love, which made us find Him whom we sought, even on this earth. When He found us alone— "He gave us His kiss, and now no one may despise us." (cf. Song of Solomon 8:1).

These divine impressions could not but bear fruit. The practice of virtue gradually became sweet and natural to me. At first my looks betrayed the effort, but, little by little, self-sacrifice seemed to come more easily and without hesitation. Our Lord has said: "To everyone that hath shall be given, and he shall abound." (Luke 19:26).

St Thérèse of Lisieux Autobiography – Page 63

Above all I endeavored to practice little hidden acts of virtue; thus I took pleasure in folding the mantles forgotten by the Sisters, and I sought for every possible occasion of helping them. One of God's gifts was a great attraction towards penance, but I was not permitted to satisfy it; the only mortification allowed me consisted in mortifying my self- love, and this did me far more good than bodily penance would have done.

St Thérèse of Lisieux Autobiography – Page 69

Jesus, too, had hidden Himself in this poor little heart, and He was pleased to show me once more the vanity of all that passes. To the great astonishment of the Community, I succeeded in painting several pictures and in writing poems which have been a help to certain souls. And just as Solomon, "turning to all the works which his hand had wrought, and to the labors wherein he had labored in vain, saw in all things vanity and vexation of mind," (cf. Ecclesiastes 2:11) so experience showed me that the sole happiness of earth consists in lying hidden, and remaining in total ignorance of created things. I understood that without love even the most brilliant deeds count for nothing. These gifts, which Our Lord lavished upon me, far from doing me any harm, drew me towards Him; I saw that He alone is unchangeable, He alone can fill the vast abyss of my desires.

St Thérèse of Lisieux Autobiography – Page 70

Now I have no desire left, unless it be to love Jesus even unto folly! It is Love alone that draws me. I no longer wish either for suffering or death, yet both are precious to me. Long did I call upon them as the messengers of joy. I have suffered much, and I have thought my barque near indeed to the Everlasting Shore. From earliest childhood I have imagined that the Little Flower would be gathered in its springtime; now, the spirit of self-abandonment alone is my guide. I have no other compass, and know not how to ask anything with eagerness, save the perfect accomplishment of God's designs upon my soul.

St Thérèse of Lisieux Autobiography – Page 86

My one interior occupation was to unite myself more and more closely to God, knowing that the rest would be given to me over and above. And indeed my hope has never been deceived; I have always found my hands filled when sustenance was needed for the souls of my Sisters. But had I done otherwise, and relied on my own strength, I should very soon have been forced to abandon my task.

St Thérèse of Lisieux Autobiography – Page 88

With me prayer is an uplifting of the heart; a glance towards heaven; a cry of gratitude and love, uttered equally in sorrow and in joy. In a word, it is something noble, supernatural, which expands my soul and unites it to God. Sometimes when I am in such a state of spiritual dryness that not a single good thought occurs to me, I say very slowly the "Our Father," or the "Hail Mary," and these prayers suffice to take me out of myself, and wonderfully refresh me.

St Thérèse of Lisieux Autobiography – Page 100

To love Thee, Jesus, is now my only desire. Great deeds are not for me; I cannot preach the Gospel or shed my blood. No matter! My brothers work in my stead, and I, a little child, stay close to the throne, and love Thee for all who are in the strife.

But how shall I show my love, since love proves itself by deeds? Well! the little child will strew flowers . . . she will embalm the Divine Throne with their fragrance, she will sing Love's Canticle in silvery tones. Yea, my

Beloved, it is thus my short life shall be spent in Thy sight. The only way I have of proving my love is to strew flowers before Thee—that is to say, I will let no tiny sacrifice pass, no look, no word. I wish to profit by the smallest actions, and to do them for Love. I wish to suffer for Love's sake, and for Love's sake even to rejoice: thus, shall I strew flowers. Not one shall I find without scattering its petals before Thee . . . and I will sing . . . I will sing always, even if my roses must be gathered from amidst thorns; and the longer and sharper the thorns, the sweeter shall be my song.

<u>My Journey with Thérèse of Lisieux</u>

Understanding the value of Charity. This is what I learned most from Thérèse, as a society we have lost our ability to have charity as part of our character. Thérèse's complete humility was like a blanket that surrounded her very being, and her innocence and gaze would shatter the very fabric of pretense.

Thérèse can ask the simplest questions, that seemed without purpose, yet in her words, in the mystery of her simplicity hid the reality of their meaning.

Who are you serving, and why are you serving them, are you serving your own agendas, your own desires, well-hidden to others, yet well known to you?

In the midst of your pursuit of God, are you seeking for the sake of fame, and fortune, what is your true motivation to know the Savior, and if your only desire is to know Him, then why all the extra stuff in your life?

Her questions cause a certain discomfort. We serve Jesus in word, but when reading His words, when we say we are living a life worthy of Jesus, are we only surrounding ourselves with comfortable people, of the same social class, and upbringing? Are we expanding our charity to the outer circle of our lives?

How will we be known by the ones who serve us, will people remember they served you at a table, because you treated them well or will you be the guest that brings tears to their eyes? These are some of the hard questions that Thérèse asked as we pondered charity and the true meaning thereof.

If the heart of the gospel is "Random Acts of Kindness", displaying the abundant life Jesus promised us, then the question becomes: "Is this a key value of my life, or am I simply sleep walking through life?"

As a people group, we need to investigate our own motivations. In a world that is overwhelmed with ego centrical ideas and individualistic approaches, are we living in charity. Knowing that the Good Shepard has given us all that we need.

QUESTIONS

1. Which part of her life do you find interesting ?

2. From the extracts out of her Autobiography, which one did you like ?

3. What does charity mean to you?

4. Is there a reason we should give to the poor, if Jesus said they will always be with you?

5. What is the difference between welfare and kindness ?

6. If we are supposed to spend time with the poor and destitute, what does this look like to you in your life ?

CHAPTER 4
Teresa of Avila

"Christ has no body now on earth but yours, no hands, no feet but yours. Yours are the eyes with which Christ looks out his compassion to the world. Yours are the feet with which he is to go about doing good. Yours are the hands with which he is to bless us now."

Teresa of Avila

Born:	1515
Died:	1582
Nationality:	Spain
Location:	Alba de Tormes
Outlook:	Carmelite Nun
Scribe & Confessor:	Fr Pedro Ibanez
Books:	Autobiography
	Life of Teresa of Jesus,
	The Interior Castle,
	Way of Perfection
	Meditations on Song of Songs
	Relationships
	Exclamaciones
	Concepts of Love
	Todas las poesías (Poems)
Interests:	Writing, Theology
Achievements:	Doctor of the Church
Key Teachings:	Accent of the Soul, Contemplative Prayer
Supernatural Miracles:	Levitation, Incorruptible body
Beatified:	24 April 1614
Canonized:	12 March 1622

The Life of Theresa

Theresa of Avila was born as Avilla, her grandfather was a Jew forced to convert to Christianity in Spain. Her father was a wool merchant, and a very wealthy businessman.

She loved reading about the saints, and on one occasion she ran away with her brother Rodrigo to the Muslim moors to find Martyrdom, enamored with the idea of dying for Jesus, her uncle having spotted them ended this errand.

Her mother died when she was 11 years old, and she was taken to the nun's school in Avilla to be educated. At the age of 18, much to her fathers and families dismay she entered the Carmelite "*Convent of the Incarnation*".

She read many of the mystics and started having mystical experiences at this time. In 1556 Jesus Christ appeared to her in bodily form, although invisible to others, He trained her for 2 years. She also had an encounter with a Seraphic angel piercing her heart during this time.

"I saw in his hand a long spear of gold, and at the point there seemed to be a little fire. He appeared to me to be thrusting it at times into my heart, and to pierce my very entrails; when he drew it out, he seemed to draw them out also, and to leave me all on fire with a great love of God. The pain was so great, that it made me moan; and yet so surpassing was the sweetness of this excessive pain, that I could not wish to be rid of it...".

Theresa was prone to Raptures which sometimes caused levitation, this was a great embracement to her, and she asked her sisters to hold her down. May city dwellers came to her convent grille where she dispensed wisdom to the community.

She became at odds with the spiritual situation of her day, and in 1562 established her own convent named "San Jose", with stricter rules of contemplation and prayer.

In 1563 she moved to the new convent house and started formulating a constitution focused on the earlier stricter monastic rules and creating a better spiritual discipline in the convent. For the first 5 years she secluded herself and focused on prayer and writing. Between 1567 – 1671 (4 year) she established convents in 7 towns based on her new order authorized by the Pope in Rome.

In 1576 she was persuaded to go into retirement as due to the persecution of her order by the church. She sent letters to King Philip of Spain, which meant her case was dropped by the Spanish inquisition.

During the last 3 years of her life, she established 5 more convents in Villanueva de la Jara in northern Andalusia (1580), Palencia (1580), Soria (1581), Burgos, and Granada (1582).

Saint Theresa of Avilla died in 1582 en-route to from Burgos to Alba de Tormes due to illness. Her last words were:

"My Lord, it is time to move on. Well then, may your will be done. O my Lord and my Spouse, the hour that I have longed for has come. It is time to meet one another".

Theology and exerts from her works

Theologians have studied the works of Theresa of Avila for centuries, in this short chapter, I only aim to give a few examples of her work, and then discuss my own experiences with her, and what she, and her life has thought me.

As stressed before, the aim of this volume is not a scholarly work, but more an introduction to the life of this spiritual heroine, to echo the words of Paul " Follow me, as I follow Christ", I believe these words echo her desire. Her legacy and significance of the Christian tradition cannot be overstated, I hope you enjoy the journey of her life, as much as I do.

Her writing on detachment from "The way of perfection" – Chapter 8

Let us now come to the detachment which we must practice, for if this is carried out perfectly it includes everything else. I say "it includes everything else" because, if we care nothing for any created things, but embrace the Creator alone, His Majesty will infuse the virtues into us in such a way that, provided we labour to the best of our abilities day by day, we shall not have to wage war much longer, for the Lord will take our defense in hand against the devils and against the whole world. Do you suppose, daughters, that it is a small benefit to obtain for ourselves this blessing of giving ourselves wholly to Him,30 and keeping nothing for ourselves? Since, as I say, all blessings are in Him, let us give Him hearty praise, sisters, for having brought us together here, where we are occupied in this alone.

The interior Castle – Page 17 – Description of the castle

I thought of the soul as resembling a castle, formed of a single diamond or a very transparent crystal, and containing many rooms, just as in heaven there are many mansions. If we reflect, sisters, we shall see that the soul of the just man is but a paradise, in which, God tells us, He takes His delight. What, do you imagine, must that dwelling be in which a King so mighty, so wise, and so pure, containing in Himself all good, can delight to rest? Nothing can be compared to the great beauty and capabilities of a soul; however keen our intellects may be, they are as unable to comprehend them as to comprehend God, for, as He has told us, He created us in His own image and likeness.

The interior Castle – Page 46 – Prayer of Recollection

The effects of divine consolations are very numerous: before describing them, I will speak of another kind of prayer which usually precedes them. I need not say much on this subject, having written about it elsewhere. This is a kind of recollection which, I believe, is supernatural. There is no occasion to retire nor to shut the eyes, nor does it depend on anything exterior; involuntarily the eyes suddenly close and solitude is found. Without any labour of one's own, the temple of which I spoke is reared for the soul in which to pray: the senses and exterior surroundings appear to lose their hold, while the spirit gradually regains its lost sovereignty. Some say the soul enters into itself; others, that it rises above itself.

I can say nothing about these terms, but had better speak of the subject as I understand it. You will probably grasp my meaning, although, perhaps, I may be the only person who understands it. Let us imagine that the senses and powers of the soul (which I compared in my allegory to the inhabitants of the castle) have fled and joined the enemy outside. After long days and years of absence, perceiving how great has been their loss, they return to the neighbourhood of the castle, but cannot manage to re-enter it, for their evil habits are hard to break off; still, they are no longer traitors, and they wander about outside.

The interior Castle – Page 46 – Prayer of Union

He will have it all in proportion to what you know you have given will your reward be great or small. There is no more certain sign whether or not we have reached the prayer of union. Do not imagine that this state of prayer is, like the one preceding it, a sort of drowsiness (I call it 'drowsiness' because the soul seems to slumber, being neither quite asleep nor wholly awake). In the prayer of union the soul is asleep, fast asleep, as regards the world and itself: in fact, during the short time this state lasts it is deprived of all feeling whatever, being unable to think on any subject, even if it wished. No effort is needed here to suspend the thoughts: if the soul can love it knows not how, nor whom it loves, nor what it desires. In fact, it has died entirely to this world, to live more truly than ever in God. This is a delicious death, for the soul is deprived of the faculties it exercised while in the body

Words of warning to those who need honor from others from "The way of perfection" – Chapter 12, Page 50

God deliver us from people who wish to serve Him yet who are mindful of their own honour. Reflect how little they gain from this; for, as I have said, the very act of desiring honour robs us of it, especially in matters of precedence: there is no poison in the world which is so fatal to perfection. You will say that these are little things which have to do with human nature and are not worth troubling about; do not trifle with them, for in religious houses they spread like foam on water, and there is no small matter so extremely dangerous as are punctiliousness about honour and sensitiveness to insult.

Being blamed by others and being innocent of the charge from "The way of perfection" – Chapter 15, Page 55

It is a great help to meditate upon the great gain which in any case this is bound to bring us, and to realize how, properly speaking, we can never be blamed unjustly, since we are always full of faults, and a just man falls seven times a day, so that it would be a falsehood for us to say we have no sin. If, then, we are not to blame for the thing that we are accused of, we are never wholly without blame in the way that our good Jesus was.

The journey of prayer from "The way of perfection" – Chapter 21, Page 72

Do not be dismayed, daughters, at the number of things which you have to consider before setting out on this Divine journey, which is the royal road to Heaven. By taking this road we gain such precious treasures that it is no wonder if the cost seems to us a high one. The time will come when we shall realize that all we have paid has been nothing at all by comparison with the greatness of our prize.

Approaching God in the Fear of the Lord from "The way of perfection" – Chapter 22, Page 77

When you approach God, then, try to think and realize Whom you are about to address and continue to do so while you are addressing Him. If we had a thousand lives, we should never fully understand how this Lord merits that we behave toward Him, before Whom even the angels tremble. He orders all things and He can do all things: with Him to will is to perform. It will be right, then, daughters, for us to endeavour to rejoice in these wondrous qualities of our Spouse and to know Whom we have wedded and what our lives should be.

The Interior Castle – Page 98 – Prayer of Joy

Amongst these favours, at once painful and pleasant, Our Lord sometimes causes in the soul a certain jubilation and a strange and mysterious kind of prayer. If He bestows this grace on you, praise Him fervently for it; I describe it so that you may know that it is something real. I believe that the faculties of the soul are closely united to God but that He leaves them at liberty to rejoice in their happiness together with the senses, although they do not know what they are enjoying nor how they do so. This may sound nonsense but it really happens. So excessive is its jubilee that the soul will not enjoy it alone but speaks of it to all around so that they may help it to praise God, which is its one desire.

Oh, what rejoicings would this person utter and what demonstrations would she make, if possible, so that all might know her happiness! She seems to have found herself again and wishes, like the father of the prodigal son, to invite all her friends to feast with her and to see her soul in its rightful place, because (at least for the time being) she cannot doubt its security.

The Interior Castle- Page 109 – Intellectual vision

His Majesty has far higher ways of communicating Himself to the soul; they are less dangerous for I do not think the evil spirit can imitate them. They are more difficult to explain, being more abstruse; therefore imaginary visions are easier to describe. God is sometimes pleased, while a person is engaged in prayer and in perfect possession of her senses, to suspend them and to discover sublime mysteries to her which she appears to see within God Himself. This is no vision of the most sacred Humanity nor can I rightly say the soul 'sees,' for it sees nothing; this is no imaginary vision but a highly intellectual one, wherein is manifested how all things are beheld in God and how He contains them within Himself. It is of great value, for although passing in an instant, it remains deeply engraved in the memory.

The interior Castle – 121 – The presence chamber

When our Lord is pleased to take pity on the sufferings, both past and present, endured through her longing for Him by this soul which He has spiritually taken for His bride, He, before consummating the celestial marriage, brings her into this His mansion or presence chamber. This is the seventh Mansion, for as He has a dwelling-place in heaven, so has He in the soul, where none but He may abide and which may be termed a second heaven.

It is important, sisters, that we should not fancy the soul to be in darkness. As we are accustomed to believe there is no light but that which is exterior, we imagine that the soul is wrapped in obscurity. This is indeed the case with a soul out of the state of grace, not, however, through any defer in the Sun of Justice which remains within it and gives it being, but the soul itself is incapable of receiving the light, as I think I said in speaking of the first Mansion.

My experience with Theresa of Avila

My journey with Theresa of Avila started while learning about the history of the church, and the mystical tradition, her books have been seen in theological circles as spiritual classics.

This journey came into a greater focus once I went to Spain on a retreat and started reading and believing some of these experiences of the saint might be available to me personally.

The following year, after attending another retreat, I went on a pilgrimage to Avila to see and experience the places she came from and walk in her footsteps like so many do. In a small church in Avila, Theresa walked up to me, and introduced herself in the realm of the spirit. I was busy praying about ecstasy and asking the Holy Spirit to bring this grace back to the Church at large.

I was taken back to the time of Theresa and saw how she patiently taught the sisters of the monastery the revelations God gave her. She was very precise and detailed about her descriptions of the mystical method of prayer, and I realized she loved each woman in a unique way, she tried to explain with great effort to help them along the way.

As I took up the assignment to write this book, she came to me again, as I was busy writing. She showed me the paths of prayer I was learning about, and the mansions of the soul she wrote about in her book. I saw the pathway, and then many road signs along the way, but her signs were like flowers, it looked like somebody took a paint brush, and painted ornate flowers and little mysteries into the road signs, one could hardly see the original sign any more, but the meaning was even more clear with all the drawing and beautiful details she added with her art.

She explained to me, "People need to see the way, they need to experience the way, almost before they can walk in the way they need to journey towards the Lord ". I understood that her teaching was almost like a travel guide, helping us not to get lost along the way, and showing us images of the road ahead.

Theresa also explained that her writing on union was based on her own time, and their own ability to communicate about the subject. She was not able to marry due to their monastic system, this then inhibited her from understanding and explaining to union in the context of marriage. She explained that sexuality helps to educate the soul in union and prepare the soul for union with God.

The spiritual union with God is completely different to the union in marriage, the scripture does however draw a parallel.

> Eph 5:22-25 NIV

> "Husbands, love your wives, just as Christ also loved the church and gave Himself for her".

This does not mean the unmarried person cannot understand union, however the process of union with God takes a bit longer to master, as the soul is not accustomed to the energetic frequency of union in higher dimensions.

She also explained the stages of prayer should not be used like a recipe book, like many have tried to use it, but rather as a guide to something much deeper, the responsibility of the teacher to train others in this way is immense, and showing others this path, comes with responsibility. Rapture without relationship would create vain imaginations of self, that brings the souls to degradation.

> 2 Cor 10:5 NIV

> "Casting down imaginations, and every high thing that exalted itself against the knowledge of God and bringing into captivity every thought to the obedience of Christ".

She is very concerned with our societies lack of caring for the poor, our inability to see actions as spiritual interlinked realities. She commented to me on how much time we spend in silence in front of screens, yet when the screen is taken away, our ability to access solitude and silence is so limited. *"The noise of the temporal has become so deafening, that men no longer hear the call of the eternal".*

Theresa also explained the reason behind penitence, something my Pentecostal mindset has lots of trouble with. Although her effort was just to say, the point to penitence is not payment for sin, or an effort to add works to the finished work of Christ, the aim is the "now", the ability to be in the present moment, and understand the weight of the divine. To quote:

"There exists only the present instant... a Now which always and without end is itself new. There is no yesterday nor any tomorrow, but only Now, as it was a thousand years ago and as it will be a thousand years hence". Meister Eckhart

She continued to say, when we separate work from worship, sacred from secular, we believe the world to be in duality, we believe some parts of creation to be more spiritual and valuable than others.

If we see the whole of nature, everything around us as a flow from the divine into this emanation, we realize, matter and reality is just as spiritual, and just as elevated, as our perceived spiritual experiences or "favors" as she calls them.

On another day while writing, Theresa came to me to discuss my understanding of prayer, I had always thought of prayer in distinct categories, with the main idea of speaking to God, and God communicating to me, His divine ideas.

While speaking with her, she explained that prayer is more than a mental state of the mind, or an emotional positioning of the heart, prayer needs to become a place of being, a place of existence. She showed me God's relationship with Adam, God came to Adam in the wind, the wind was not a cool breeze as we understand, the cool breeze was a realm of energetic existence, that created relationship, understanding and union. In the place where Adam and God met, was not just a place in the Garden, it was a modality of conversation, a realm or a dimension where understanding flowed between the divine, and the created being.

This place where the Creator and the creation, could intermingle, interweave, and become understood by each other. She also explained why Jesus was in the Garden, Jesus became the one who stood in the garden again, releasing His will, to the divine will.

In a sense, Jesus became every man, in the garden, Jesus stood as the tree of life, building a place in the spiritual dimension, where God could once again, intermingle with creation, where the Last Adam, became the First Adam, so that we could inherit the kingdom of relationship, and bare fruits from the tree of life. This tree would now last for eternity, and every other tree of knowledge or self-effort of man, would now be removed, and bare no fruit in the presence of the Holy God.

Prayer for Theresa was not just about the mystical prayer methods of contemplation, or recollection, or even the higher dimensions of prayer, for her, being in a constant place of prayer, meant she had a realm of prayer, built around her awareness, in a sense never leaving the inner prayer room of her heart, always standing and ministering before the Throne of the Father.

QUESTIONS

1. Which part of her life did you find thought provoking ?

2. Out of the extract from her writings did you enjoy ?

3. What does prayer mean to you ?

4. How do you live a life or prayer

CHAPTER 5
Bridget of Sweden

"To write well and speak well is mere vanity if one does not live well."

Bridget of Sweden

Born:	1303
Died:	23 July 1373
Nationality:	Uppland, Sweden
Location:	Rome
Outlook:	Catholic
Books:	Autobiography
Interests:	Pilgrimage to Rome
Achievements:	Establishment of monastic order (Brigittines)
Key Teachings:	Caring for the poor, Prophecy and Revelations, Passions of the Cross, Nativity of Jesus, Sacred heart of Jesus, Purgatory
Canonized:	7 October 1391

The Life of Bridget of Sweden

Bridget of Sweden was born on 1303 in Uppland in Sweden to a very wealthy family. Her father, Birger Persson of the Finsta family, was a governor and law-speaker, and a wealthy landowner. Her mother was related to the Swedish king of the time.

At the age of 14 she married Ulf Gudmarsson, (Lord of Narke), and bore 8 children of which 6 survived childhood. The queen of Sweden, (Blanch of Namur), asked her to be the lady in waiting in her early thirties.

In 1341 she and her husband went on a pilgrimage to Santiago de Compostela in Spain. After returning to Sweden, her husband died and she became a member of the Third order of St. Francis, to focus on serving the poor and destitute for the rest of her life.

She established a double monastery at Vadstena called the "Order of the most Holy Savior", also called the Brigantines. These communities included both men and women in a joint worship service, with separate living quarters in cloisters. King Magnus of Sweden supported these monasteries financially and politically.

In 1350, Bridget went on pilgrimage to Rome, the aim of this trip was to obtain papal sanction for her order. Due to the Pope residing in the French city of Avignon, she had to wait until 1370 for the final approval from Pope Urban V.

Bridget remained in Rome until her death in 1373. She never returned to Sweden, and her love and care for the Italian church has made her a household name in the city, well known for her care for the poor and her kindness towards others.

Theology and Exerts from Bridget's Works

Bridget's theology is one of suffering, pain and loss, she sees Jesus being crucified here and today, in a sense every day, and our response to this crucifixion is our daily life.

Prophecies and Revelations – Page 60, Chapter 38

The Father spoke to the Son, saying: "I came with love to the Virgin and took your true body from her. You are therefore in me and I in you. Just as fire and heat are never separated, so it is impossible to separate the Divinity from the Manhood." The Son answered: "May all glory and honour be to you Father; may your will be done in me and mine in you." The Father answered him again: "Behold, my Son, I am entrusting this new bride to you like a sheep to be guided and educated. As the owner of the sheep, you will get from her cheese to eat and milk to drink and wool to clothe yourself with. But you, bride, should obey him. You have three things you must do: you have to be patient, obedient and willing to do what is good."

Prophecies and Revelations – Page 128, Chapter 11 of Book 2

His soul saw it all and said to itself in exultation: 'Happy am I to have been created! Happy am I to have served my God whom I now behold! Happy am I, for I have joy and glory that will never end!' In such a way did my friend come to me and receive such a reward. Although not everyone sheds his blood for the sake of my name, nevertheless, everyone will receive the same reward, provided they have the intention of giving their lives for me if the occasion presents itself and the needs of the faith demand it. See how important a good intention is!"

Prophecies and Revelations – Page 145

You do not see the sight you see as it is in fact. For if you saw the spiritual beauty of the angels and of holy souls, your body could not bear to see it but would break like a vessel, broken and decayed due to the soul's joy at the sight. If you saw the demons as they are, you would either go on living in great sorrow or you would die a sudden death at the terrible sight of them. This is why spiritual beings appear to you as if they had bodies.

Prophecies and Revelations – Page 224

Love is true when you love God with all your heart and affections, when you take the glory and fear of God into prior consideration in all your actions, when you commit not the least little sin while trusting to your good deeds, when you practice temperance prudently without growing weak from too much fervour, when you do not have an inclination to sin out of cowardice or ignorance of temptations. Love is perfect when nothing is as enjoyable to a person as God.

Prophecies and Revelations – Page 232, Chapter 1 of Book 4

A male person appeared to the bride. His hair seemed as if shorn with reproach; his body was drenched in oil and completely naked, though he was in no way ashamed. He said to the bride:" The scripture, which you call holy, says that no good deed will go unrewarded. This is the scripture that is known for you as the Bible but which, for us, is as bright as the sun, incomparably more splendid than gold, bearing fruit like the seed that produces fruit a hundredfold. Just as gold excels other metals, so the scripture, which you say is Holy though we call it Golden, excels all other books, because in it the true God is glorified and announced, the deeds of the patriarchs are unfolded, the inspirations of the prophets are explained.

Prophecies and Revelations – Page 305, The Clothes of Moses

Why did I reveal such magnificence in material vestments to Moses? It was, of course, in order to use them to teach and symbolize the magnificence and beauty of the soul. As the vestments of the priests were seven in number, so too the soul that approaches the body of God should have seven virtues without which there is no salvation. The first vestment of the soul, then, is contrition and confession. These cover the head. The second is desire for God and desire for chastity. The third is work in honour of God as well as patience in adversity. The fourth is caring neither for human praise nor reproach but for the honour of God alone. The fifth is abstinence of the flesh along with true humility. The sixth is consideration of the favours of God as well as fear of his judgments. The seventh is love of God above all things and perseverance in good undertakings.

My experience with Saint Bridget of Sweden

Saint Bridget: a very humble lady, her demeanor is sober and her eyes piercing blue orbs of light. She speaks in soft tones, and as the words settle in your heart, the deep purity of her thoughts starts to enlighten your heart, bringing clarity to very complicated concepts.

She spoke to me about the nature of morality and how we are confusing the character of Christ for an elevated sense of morality and self-righteousness.

In a society where people spend their lives taking selfies, focusing on social media, and keeping up appearances, we have become focused on the outward show of Christianity and very little on our ability to act more Christlike.

Matt 23:25 NIV

"Woe to you, teachers of the law and Pharisees, you hypocrites!
You clean the outside of the cup and dish, but inside they are
full of greed and self-indulgence."

She quoted this verse to me, showing how our idea of morality changes based on the culture. Things become "morally acceptable" as the surrounding society changes. For example, the Amish community: they have kept their morality and values as the founding fathers prescribed them and are still dressing and acting that way. This then is indicative of what they consider as acceptable and it has not changed with the pressure of society.

Ethics is described as "moral principles that govern a person's behavior or the conducting of an activity".

We know ethics, or a certain code of ethics, exists for most civilizations. In certain societies also considered the moral law. The problem with morals and ethics is that it still is very subjective and based on a fixed understanding of situations arising in a specific culture.

The nature of "right and wrong" or a dualistic thinking systems, and moral philosophy is the perceptions that these rules are fixed and eternal; however the tree of knowledge is also based on the same system – a system that brings death and destruction.

What Bridget was trying to convey is when somebody says, "it's second nature", what then is the first nature? The reality is that Jesus came to change our whole nature, a single nature, that demands another character, where our decisions are based.

1 Cor 10:23 ESV

"All things are lawful, but not all things are helpful. All things
are lawful, but not all things build up."

The question then becomes: Am I acting according to the new nature that Jesus gave me; not just what Jesus would do, but how would Jesus think. Knowing not just the actions but understanding the motivation of God, the "ways" of God. Spiritual maturity is only achieved when we start acting congruently to the nature of the Father, we say we know.

The woman caught in idolatry was convicted by the culture and law to death, but Christ carrying the character of One who forgives and shows mercy, ministers life to her and frees her from her sin imprisonment and the moral code dictated by the law.

In the same way, Jesus extended healing to a man on the sabbath. Moral law dictated a certain protocol, but Jesus prioritizes human need with a character of love.

Character is built in various ways, a lot of the time through challenges and problems that we are faced with. We need to embrace these situations to allow the divine process of character building cushioned by the yoke of intimacy to create the divine nature of God inside of us.

This molding of the human nature into the new nature allows the potentiality for humanity to become like Jesus. Where our first nature is not anymore to give into a sinful reactive response to life and situation, but the benevolent actions of mature Christlike sons.

You have a responsibly to speak, act and love the way Jesus loved people, Jesus does not condemn, or even act the way the community of His day predicts. He insists on surrounding himself with the poor, the lost and the broken. He finds ways to integrated society, He moves His disciples from their comfortable fishing boats, to the taverns of Jerusalem where the sinners are, ridiculed as a wine bibber, He chooses the company of the broken, addict, and shows the heart of God in every situation.

The ministry of Jesus was offensive to the pharisees of His day, but it made His own disciples even more uncomfortable. Are we prepared to step into the uncomfortable new nature where character dictates and love rules.

QUESTIONS

1. Which part of her life did you enjoy the most ?

2. From the Extract of " Prophecies and Revelations " which part did you enjoy the most and why ?

3. Do you think the soul can be transformed ?

4. Which parts of your soul would you like so see changed ?

5. Do you have a plan to mature your soul, and what is the normal process God uses to mature the soul ?

CHAPTER 6
Saint Catherine of Genoa

*My "me" is God nor do I recognize
any other "me" except my God
himself.*

Catherine of Genoa

Born:	1447
Died:	1510
Nationality:	Italy
Location:	Genoa (Italy)
Outlook:	Catholic
Scribe & Confessor:	Father Marabotti
Books:	Book of the marvelous life and holy teaching of the Blessed Catherine of Genoa
Interests:	Mystic, writer, visionary
Achievements:	Manager of the hospital
Key Teachings:	The soul, body and spirit
Beatified:	1675
Canonized:	1737

The Life of Catherine of Genoa

Catherine was born in 1447 in Genoa, Italy. She was the youngest child of 5 children and her noble Fieschi family were close to the Pope of the time. Her father was the Viceroy of Naples.

At the age of 13 she wanted to enter a convent, but she was denied based on her youth, and at the age of 16 married Giuliano Adorno, a noble local. He was a terrible husband, and they had no children in their marriage. After 10 years of marriage she converted on 22 March 1473 after a mystical experience with God.

She served the sick in the hospital of Genoa. Catherine's husband subsequently converted as well and joined her in her service.

They lived at the Pammatone, a local hospital, her husband became a Franciscan, but Catherine never joined no formal church order. Her husband's spending ruined them financially, and she later became the manager and treasurer of the hospital.

She died on 15 September 1510, from exhaustion and over exertion in her service and charity to the poor and the sick.

Catherine's Doctrine

I have chosen some excerpts from her work to show in her words some of what she believed; however, these works being translated from the Italian original may be open to more interpretation.

Our aim in this section is to describe, and show some of her works, her thoughts and her revelations, as they stand on their own.

Ideas on Union and Self righteousness

Wherefore, it is necessary that the soul which desires to be preserved from sin in this life, and to glorify God in the other, should be spotless, pure, and simple, and not voluntarily retain a single thing which is not purged by contrition, confession and satisfaction, because all our works are imperfect and defective. Whence, if I consider and observe clearly, with the interior eye, I see that I ought to live entirely detached from self; Love has wished me to understand this, and in a manner I do understand it, so that I could not possibly be deceived; and for my part I have so abandoned myself, that I can regard it only as a demon, or worse, if I may so say.

After God has given a soul the light in which she perceives the truth that she cannot even will, and much less work, apart from him, without always soiling and making turbid the clear waters of his grace, then she sacrifices all to him, and he takes possession of his creature, and both inwardly and outwardly occupies her with himself, so that she can do nothing but as her sweet Love wills. Then the soul, by reason of its union with God, contradicts Him in nothing, nor does aught but what is pure, upright, gentle, sweet, and delightful, because God allows nothing to molest it. And these are the works which please the Lord our God.

The Goodness of God

"I saw," said she, "a sight which greatly consoled me. I was shown the living source of goodness in God, as it was when yet alone and unparticipated in by any creature. Then I saw it begin to communicate itself to the creatures, and it did so to the fair company of angels, in order to give them the fruition of its own ineffable glory, demanding no other return from them than that they should recognize themselves as creatures, created by the supreme goodness, and having their being wholly from God, apart from whom all things are reduced to pure nonentity. The same must be said of the soul, which also was created immortal, that it might attain to beatitude; for if there were no immortality there could be no happiness. And because the angels were incapable of annihilation, therefore when their pride and disobedience robed them in the vesture of sin, God deprived them of that participation in his goodness, which, by his grace, he had ordained to give them: hence they remained so infernal and terrible that none, even of those who are specially enlightened by God, can possibly conceive their degradation. He did not, however, subtract all his mercy from them, for had he done so, they would be still more malicious, and would have a hell as infinitely immense in torture as it is in duration."

Thoughts on Transformation of the Soul

When the good God calls us in this world, he finds us full of vices and sins, and his first work is to give us the instinct to practice virtue; then he incites us to desire perfection, and afterwards, by infused grace, he conducts us to the true annihilation, and finally to the true transformation. This is the extraordinary road along which God conducts the soul. But when the soul is thus annihilated and transformed, it no longer works, or speaks, or wills, or feels, or understands, nor has it in itself any knowledge, either of that which is internal or external, which could possibly affect it; and, in all these things God is its director and guide without the help of any creature.

In this state, the soul is in such peace and tranquillity that it seems to her that both soul and body are immersed in a sea of the profoundest peace, from which she would not issue for anything that could happen in this life.

Pure Love that Transcends the Mind

The true and pure love is of such force that it cannot be diverted from its object, nor can it see or feel anything else. Hence it is useless toil to try to make such creatures employ themselves in the things of this world, for with regard to them they are as insensible as if they were dead.

It is impossible to describe this love in words or figures which will not, in comparison with the reality, seem entirely false. This only can be understood, namely, that the human intellect is unable to comprehend it. And to him who seeks to know what it is that I know and feel, I can only reply that it transcends all utterance.

Flames of Divine Love

But there is this difference between material fire and the flames of divine love, that the one consumes and destroys, while the other sustains and strengthens.

Divine Pure Love towards Us

She saw, too, a ray of his mercy shining into hell; for the wicked deserve infinite punishment for an infinite time; but the divine mercy has made the time only infinite, but has limited the extent of the punishment, and therefore a greater one might justly have been inflicted.

This Soul also beheld a certain ray of love issuing from that divine fountain, and darting towards man with a force as if to annihilate him; and she saw that when it found impediments, then, if it were possible for God to feel pain, he would suffer the greatest of all grief. This ray aimed only to penetrate the soul, and it was her own fault if she were not penetrated by it, for the ray surrounded her on all sides, seeking entrance; but the soul, blinded by self-love, did not perceive it. And when God saw a soul self-condemned, who through her wilfulness would not give entrance to the light, he seemed to say: "So great is the love which I bear to this soul, that I desire never to abandon her."

The Mercy of Divine Love

These two visions never again faded away from her memory, and the one revealed to her the other; for, beholding the infinite mercy of God performing such works of pure love towards man, the Soul would have fainted from excess of delight if any more had been manifested to her. Such a vision, moreover, made clear to her the malice of man, seeing that great love of God continually employed in her behalf, almost, as it were, in spite of herself; for God, looking not at the sins that she committed, never ceased in his mercy to do her good in many ways, being moved by none of her offences but rather with pure love repairing them, always watchful for her benefit.

The Sea of Divine Pure Love

This work God effects by love alone, which is so great that it is incessantly seeking the profit and advantage of this Soul, his beloved.

But the special work of which I speak, God performs without the aid of the Soul, and in the following manner: he fills her with a secret love, which deprives her of her natural life, so that the work carried on in her is wholly supernatural. She remains meanwhile in that sea of secret love which is so great that all who are drawn within it sink overwhelmed, for it overpowers the memory, the understanding, and the will: and to these powers, thus submerged in the divine love, all things else which approached them would be their hell, for they have been deprived of the natural life for which she Soul was created.

Such a soul, while yet in this life, shares, in some degree, the happiness of the blessed; but this is hidden even from herself, for it is so great and high that she is unable to comprehend it, exceeding as it does the capacity of her powers, which look to nothing beyond, but rest satisfied and submerged in this sea of love.

The unknowable love of the divine – God incomprehensible

For love is God himself, who cannot be comprehended, except by the wonderful effects of the great love which he is ever manifesting, and which can neither be estimated nor imagined. and then I reveal to the Soul but one spark of my pure love, she is constrained to return me that love, whose power compels her to do her all for me, even, if need were, to suffer torture and a thousand deaths. How much love may be infused into the hearts of men, can be learned from what men have done for love of me. But I see, my beloved, that thou seekest not this operative love in its effects, but those gentle drops that I pour into the hearts of my elect, and which melt the Soul, the Spirit, and even the bodily powers, so that they act no longer. By these drops the Soul remains immersed in the sweetness of that love, and is incapable of performing any action

Experiences with Catherine of Genoa

Catherine appeared to me as a typical Italian woman. She had an interesting way of explaining how our likes, and our dislikes from a lattice work in front of our spiritual eyes, this would then create our reality and our experience. So much of our likes and dislikes are formed by our consumer and material lifestyle.

In some sense our own preferences became a prison, not allowing us to experience life outside of our own personal needs and desires. In time, this created a perspective of the spiritual dimension, which made people seem blind to the very basic obstacles in front of their eyes.

Our greatest disability as our lack of ability to see beyond ourselves. We become self-obsessed and focused on the time and place we are living in as the most fundamental reality to relate to the world around us.

I saw how my own absorption with Time and Space (Locality and Milieu), created a spiritual blindness that locked me into a loop of life.

As she removed this way of seeing with Jesus, my eyes and ears opened to the possibilities in God's heart, and the experiences once considered sacred and secular merged into a more holistic viewpoint.

I saw how Jesus moved me beyond my self-preservation, and into an eternal reality, where lack, fear and deadlines seem to mean little more than figments of my own making. The glasses on my eyes were creating shadows and images, but the reality of the spiritual dimensions looked very different without these pre-conceived ideas.

As I encountered her, the one thing this saint taught me was not the technical nature of my soul in relation to my body and spirit, or any of her basic theology, but to start doing things out of my own box. I saw how she looked at our time in history, as a pivotal point in humanity and Christianity, we are standing at a crossroads, and our choices in this era might determine more in future than we currently believe. Can we carry the consuming love of and for God to step into a place of choice? Where the choices we make are based in eternity.

The passion of the mystics cannot be overstated, the physical burning sensations she experienced as a manifestation of love, seems extreme to the modern mind, yet the burning seraphic nature of her being consumed her with the Love of God.

This love needs to infiltrate the very dimensions of our soul realities and structures. This includes the nature of the carnal soul, the fallen soul, the memories of sin in the body, and the sin nature in the old soul. The new soul, created by God, as we are born again, form a substance around the believer that emanates this divine love.

The soul is very much like the breastplate worn by the high priest, the divine qualities like humility and patience start shining as Christ becomes the light in our hearts, the breastplate we wear lights up the world in colors around us, to bring humanity to a higher revelation of His divine love.

We are the new priesthood according to 1 Peter 2:9, "But you are a chosen people, a Royal priesthood, a holy nation, a peculiar people".

As a chosen people we need to manifest the eternity that lives in our hearts. We need to love, and make choices fitting to a future generation that will want to know God.

QUESTIONS

1.   What part of her life disturbs you the most ?

2.   From the extracts of her writings, which part did you enjoy ?

3.   Do you think everybody sees the world the same ?

4.   How do we know what is true, if we can't trust our thoughts or senses ?

5.   IF we have blind spots in our perception of reality, how do we fix these blind spots ?

6.   Have you observed how you react to somebody, without trying to change your actions from a third person perspective or are you just reacting to life ?

CHAPTER 7
Hildegard of Bingen

"Humanity take a good look at yourself. Inside, you've got heaven and earth, and all of creation. You're a world. Everything is hidden in you."

Hildegard of Bingen

Born: 1098

Died: 1179

Nationality: German

Location: Rupertsberg

Outlook: Benedictine Abbess

Scribe & Confessor: Volmar

Books: Scivias
                    ("Know the ways ")

Liber Vitae Meritorum ("Book of Life's Merits"
or "Book of the Rewards of Life", composed
115–1163)

Liber Divinorum Operum ("Book of Divine
Works", also known as De operatione Dei, "On
God's Activity", composed 1163/4–1172 or
1174)

Interests: Writer, Composter,
                    Philosopher, Inventor,
                    Medicine, Theologian,
                    Polymath

Achievements: Doctor of the Church,
                    Medical work,
                    Musical work

Key Teachings: Life After Death,
                    Practical guide to life,
                    Theology, Creation

Supernatural Miracles: Mystical vision,
                    Ecstatic visions

Beatified: 26 August 1326

Canonized: 10 May 2012

The Life of Hildegard

Hildegard was born during 1098 in Bermersheim vor der Höhe, County Palatine of the Rhine, Germany to a free lower nobility family in service of Count Meginhard of Sponheim. Hildegard was the youngest of 10 children, and although she was quite sick from birth, Hildegard had mystical visions from a very young age.

She stayed at the Benedictine monastery in Disibodenberg where she was placed in the care of a nun, Jutta, from the age of 8 until she was 14 when she was enclosed as a nun and took her vows. Jutta taught her how to read and write, skills normally withheld from women in the middle ages except for nobility.

When Jutta died in 1136, Hildegard was elected Magistrate of the community of nuns by her fellow sisters.

Hildegard and 20 nuns moved to the St. Rupertsberg monastery in 1150, where Volmar served as provost, as well as Hildegard's confessor and scribe. In 1165 Hildegard founded a second monastery for her nuns at Eibingen

In 1141 at the age of 42, Hildegard received a vision from God, asking her to write down her visions, these visions she kept private for the first 40 years of her life, only sharing them with Jutta.

Hildegard writes:

"But I, though I saw and heard these things, refused to write for a long time through doubt and bad opinion and the diversity of human words, not with stubbornness but in the exercise of humility, until, laid low by the scourge of God, I fell upon a bed of sickness; then, compelled at last by many illnesses, and by the witness of a certain noble maiden of good conduct [the nun Richardis von Stade] and of that man whom I had secretly sought and found, as mentioned above, I set my hand to the writing. While I was doing it, I sensed, as I mentioned before, the deep profundity of scriptural exposition; and, raising myself from illness by the strength I received, I brought this work to a close – though just barely – in ten years. (...) And I spoke and wrote these things not by the invention of my heart or that of any other

person, but as by the secret mysteries of God I heard and received them in the heavenly places. And again, I heard a voice from Heaven saying to me, 'Cry out, therefore, and write thus!'"

Hildegard is known as a Polymath (a person of wide knowledge or learning), and thus, she wrote works on Theology, Doctrine, Medicine and Science. She also invited her own language, which was spoken by the nuns in the convents she founded, as a secret language. This language "Lingua Ignota" was used to unite the nuns living together and give them a sense of their own social structure.

She is considered the founder of scientific natural history in Germany, with all the work she did in the medicinal field of the study of herbs and plants.

Hildegard composed Ordo Virtutum (Play of the Virtues) which included 82 songs she composed, a prolific composer of her era, she also composed some liturgical works for church worship and praise services.

Hildegard died on 17 September 1179 (aged 81) in Bingen am Rhein, County Palatine of the Rhine, Holy Roman Empire of the time.

The nuns claimed they saw two streams of light appear in the skies and cross over the room where she was dying.

The Visions of Hildegard

Hildegard had many visions and divine experiences and to express her in this book fully would not be possible, she wrote about 400 letters to many influential leaders, politicians and even the pope of her time.

She explained her interest in cosmology and many other fields of study (too many to mention), a truly intellectual giant of her time.

The focus of the extracts' below will be more on her visionary experiences as written in her works, not to interpret them, but to see them in all their glory, for what they are.

The Spirit of the fear of the Lord – Page 152, The Iron Mountain (Scivias1, 1)

"And before this figure, at the roots of the mountain, there stood an image covered with eyes, and because of the eyes I could not make out the human form beneath."

The 'image covered with eyes' represents fear of the Lord in the presence of God. She contemplates the kingdom of God in all humility. Covered with the discernment of good and fair intentions, she practices enthusiasm and constancy in human behaviour. And this is why you cannot see the human form beneath the cover of the discerning eyes: because her sharp-sighted gaze dispels all the obliviousness to God's justice which human beings often feel in their jaded hearts. And her vigilance is such that it cannot be diverted by the weakness of mortal inquiry.

The Man Looking East and South – Page 154, The Book of Life's Merits I

Now his face shone with such splendor that I could not perfectly see it. The white cloud was near his mouth in the likeness of a trumpet, full of the rapid soundings of all musical sounds, and when the man blew a breath, it sent out three winds: one bore a cloud of fire; one bore a cloud of storms; one bore a cloud of light. And each cloud was supported by its wind.

While the wind bearing the cloud of fire remained before the man's face, the other two winds descended with their clouds to his chest, and there they expanded their breath outwards. But the wind that had stayed before the man's face extended its cloud from the East to the South.

In the cloud of fire were myriads of fiery beings; and they were all one life, in one will and one conjunction. And in their presence a writing table was laid out, filled with feathers. The tablet soared in the precepts of God when the precepts of God bore it aloft. And the knowledge of God had inscribed hidden mysteries upon it which the myriads of beings observed with one unified devotion. And when they had studied what was written the divine virtue came upon them and like a single mighty trumpet, they sounded forth with one sound in all varieties of music.

A Vision of Love – Page 179, The Book of Divine Works I

The figure spoke: "I am the supreme fire and energy. I have kindled all the sparks of the living, and I have breathed out no mortal things, for I judge them as they are. I have properly ordained the cosmos, flying about the circling circle with my upper wings, that is with wisdom. I am the fiery life of divine substance, I blaze above the beauty of the fields, I shine in the waters, I burn in sun, moon, and stars. And I awaken all to life with every wind of the air, as with invisible life that sustains everything. For the air lives in greenness and fecundity. The waters flow as though they are alive. The sun also lives in its own light, and when the moon has waned it is rekindled by the light of the sun and thus lives again; and the stars shine out in their own light as though they are alive.

I established the pillars that support the whole circle of the earth. I made the winds, and, subject to them, the wings of the winds, which are lesser winds. Through their gentle force, these contain the stronger winds and prevent them from showing their full strength with great danger; in the same way the body covers the soul and contains it lest it breathe out and expire. And conversely also, just as the breath of the soul strengthens and sustains the body so that it does not weaken, in the same way the stronger winds energize the subsidiary winds to carry out their appropriate tasks.

Thus, I am concealed in things as fiery energy. They are ablaze through me, like the breath that ceaselessly enlivens the human being, or like the wind-tossed flame in a fire. All these things live in their essence, and there is no death in them, for I am life."

Learning with Hildegard

During the time that I studied Hildegard's life and works I attended a work conference. Sometime into the conference I could sense that Hildegard wanted to engage with me. Images and drawings about time and the soul began to fill my spirit.

While drawing some of these images, trying to make sense of what I was seeing, Hildegard explained the infrastructure of the soul, as the soul exists in this reality, and then the architecture of our inner space, as a manifestation of God in our current society.

Architecture of the inner space:

- New Soul – Greek work Kinos

  The new soul is created at the "born again" moment of the believer and creates a dimensional framework to experience God again.

- Alternating Soul

  Alternating Soul is the part of the soul which is created to interface with the "old soul fragments" in the body and then bring them to the current reality where the decision-making takes place.

- Inter-Relating Soul

  Inter-Relating Soul then is the part of the soul that can access the higher levels of consciousness and start interfacing with God on other planes of existence.

- Hyper-Soul Reality

Hyper-Soul is then the soul which is not just able to travel and navigate the spiritual dimensions, but also to perceive God outside of the normal human construct of reality. This soul is developed on higher dimensional frameworks, where energy and frequency does not exist any longer. This is on some level only a "thought "or awareness realm, where the perception is completely in the hands of God.

The human soul has the unlimited capacity to develop and mature after salvation. This realization led Hildegard to talk about time and space. That Salvation means the time and space limitation is now lost to enable access into spiritual realities.

Ecc 3:11

"He has made everything beautiful in its time. **He has also set eternity in the human heart**; yet no one can fathom what God has done from beginning to end."

Hildergard then went on to explain the nature of reality in this way:

When we look at the existence of time and space, we realize that this is created in a 3-dimensional space, some would say a cube like structure.

The intersection of time and space creates reality as we perceive and understand the world around us, to some degree the spiritual world, or the unseen world will then be a fourth dimension.

When a soul turns towards God and become "born again", a 5th dimension is opened up to this person, and the nature of the spiritual dimensions of God is then unlocked for this "Kinos Being" or New Creation as 2 Corinthians 5:17 explains.

The multidimensionality of the human soul is unlocked because of this "new soul" that God birthed into existence. This then means the human can experience other dimensions and realities outside the current time and space of his own existence.

Perception in the spiritual world, or let's use the phrase "the eyes of the heart being enlightened", is the virtue of the believer. This means that if a person carries humility, they are able to see into realms and dimensions where humility is needed to comprehend this spiritual dimension or world.

When the soul is elevated into a place of union, not just unity with God, but true union, his capacity to perceive is then located in the understanding and senses of God, which is above the realm of virtue, and character, but located in the energetic nature of reality. The frequency of the "spiritual worlds" is then unlocked because the spiritual world does not exist only because of energies, but in other places outside of time and space, where the eternal world permeates the uncreated world.

If God is limitless and timeless, it means this place where God exists has no time and has no space, this place is not based on any structure, any physical or quantum laws we understand.

The place where God exists is not a place of science or a dimension inside the created universe. We exist inside God, yet God does not exist only inside us, but every place where we are not. We are about to matter, to something that has been created. God has always been, and will always be, outside of our limitations.

Hildegard's four dimensions of time:

- Current "Now"

- Infinite "Now"

- Eternal "Now"

- History – Past (Time in solar moments, or universal time, based on the galactic center)

Current Now

The current now is explained as you experience this moment, the moment you are now reading these words, this is the current now, in a sense it is being created as we live life. The passing of time intermingled with our awareness and observation creating a conscious observation of this moment.

Infinite Now

This is the uninterrupted link we have with the future, as we are linked to it now, only a "born again" soul can experience this, as this moment is created by the individual experiencing spiritual realities outside of time, based on the infinite nature of God, yet the time interface is still needed because it impacts the current reality.

Eternal Now

This is the moment God experiences us, the moment He becomes the creative point of the soul, the moment the new soul is created, and then exists outside of time and space, in a sense this happens inside the nature of God, outside of created time, or created light. This happens inside uncreated light, before creation started, God returns to the beginning, and in essence creates the new soul from outside of creation.

History – Past

This is what we remember from the moment that passes, this is essentially a record of time, that has elapsed, not just in our memory, but in physicality.

Because we live in a time and space dimension, the effects of time, is seen on the material universe, essentially this then becomes the observation of the 3rd law of thermodynamics , which means an observation of energy loss of the system, however never a loss that degrades the complete system into annihilation.

She mentioned many times, that humanity, and our current era, is ready for expansion and vast development, like the time after she lived. She likened our time to the Renaissance and explained to me that technology is a sign of the goodness of God.

QUESTIONS

1.   Which of her interests fascinate you as well, considering she had many?

2.   Which of the extracts of her writings did you enjoy the most ?

3.   How do you think our understanding of time will change during the next 10 years ?

4.   Do you think science is opposed to God ?

CHAPTER 8
Mechthild of Magdeburg

"Lord, you are my lover,

My longing, My flowing stream,

My sun, And I am your reflection.

The day of my spiritual awakening

was the day I saw and knew I saw

all things in God and God in all
things."

Mechthild of Magdeburg.

Born:	1207
Died:	1294
Nationality:	German
Location:	Magdeburg (Germany)
Outlook:	Beguine | Dominican
Scribe & Confessor:	Henry of Halle
Books:	The Flowing Light of Divinity
Interests:	Mystic, writer, visionary, poet
Achievements:	First mystic to write in German
Key Teachings:	Purgatory, Hell, Heaven, Light from the Throne Room

The Life of Mechthild of Magdeburg

Mechthild was born to a Noble Saxon family in Germany. At the age of 12 she renounced the luster of the world and became a Beguine at Magdeburg. At the community she learned about the Dominicans and read many of their works.

A Beguine is a person, normally a lady who renounces early wealth, and spends their lives in community with others, taking care of the poor, they normally have some business intrests to help fund their charity in devours, Mechthild was known as a Beguine.

Her confessor, Henry of Halle (a Dominican), helped her to compose her life's work; "The flowing Light" or "The flowing light of Divinity".

She was a staunch activist against the church leaders and their lack of religious discipline, this led to some of her works being burned.

Amid the criticism, advancing age, and becoming blind at the age of 60, she joiner in 1272 the Cistercian nunnery in Helfta who took care of her and offered her protection. This is also where she dictated her spiritual experiences and visions and completed her writings.

This convent is also the same place where **Mechtilde of Hakeborn,** and **Gertrude the Great** lived before her.

It is unclear if she took the Cistercian vows, but it seems she died there in 1282.

Visions of Mechthild of Magdeburg

Mechthils devotional poems speak about courtly love poetry as well as folk songs. Her book is not only an account of her own experience of divine vision but a fearless condemnation of wrongs she observed in the local clergy.

The Flowing Light of the Divine Godhead – Page 29, 1 and 4

Whenever the poor soul comes to court, she is discerning and refined. Then she looks joyfully on her God. Ah how lovingly she is received there! She then falls silent and longs intensly for His praise. Then He, with great desire, shows her His divine heart. It is like red gold buring in a great coal-fire. Then He puts her into His glowing heart. When the great Lord and the little maid thus embrace and are mingled as water and whine, then she becomes nothing and is enraptured. When she can cope no longer, then He is lovesick for her, as He always was, for He neither waxes or wanes.

The Flowing Light of the Divine Godhead – Page 33, 1 and 35

The desert has 12 things:

1) *You should love nothingness*

2) *You should flee somethingness*

3) *You should stand alone*

4) *And you should go to no one*

5) *You should not be too busy*

6) *And you should stand free of all things.*

7) *You should release the bound*

8) *And restrain the free*

9) *You should tend the sick*

10) *And yet have no care for yourself*

11) *You should drink the water of suffering*

12) *And light the fire of love with the kindling of virtue:*

Then you will live in the true desert.

The Flowing Light of the Divine Godhead – Page 35, 1 and 44: Dialogue between the Mechthild and Jesus

I am a fully-grown bride, I want to go to my Love. O Lady, if you go there, then we shall be completely blinded, for the Godhead, as you well know, is so fiery hot that all the fire and incandescence, in which heaven and all the saints burn and glow, streams from His divine breath and out of His human mouth on the advice of the Holy Spirit. How could you last even an hour there?

The Flowing Light of the Divine Godhead – Page 52, 3.1: Book 3

There I saw the creation and the ordering of God's house that He Himself built with His mouth: and in it He placed what is dearest to Him that He has made with His own hands. The house that has been created is called Heaven, the choirs in it are called the Kingdom, and this taken together we speak of the Kingdom of Heaven. The composition of the Kingdom of Heaven is finite, but there will never be an end to its existence.

The Flowing Light of the Divine Godhead – Page 53, 3.1: Book 3 – Visions of the Throne Room

God's preachers and spiritual lovers come into these choirs, even if they are not virgins. Indeed they come amongst the cherubim with honor! There, without asking, I saw the reward of the preachers, as it is yet to come about. Their chairs are wonderful, their reward is special. The front legs of the chairs are two burring lights which signify true love and holy example and faithful inner resolve. The back of the chair is so pleasantly free of restraint and in blissful repose so sweet, more than one can express, in contrast to the strict obedience to which they are subject here.

The Flowing Light of the Divine Godhead – Page 54, 3.1: Book 3 – Praise to Jesus, and commitment to silence about heaven

O you lovely Lamb and delightful Young Man, Jesus, Child of the heavenly Father, when You rise up and travel though all the choirs and beckon lovingly to the virgins, then they will follow You, full of praise, into that most overwhelming place, about which I can say no more to anyone.

The Flowing Light of the Divine Godhead – Page 55, 3.1: Book 3 – Description of the choirs of heaven

God has bestowed so much splendor on the choirs of Heaven, that I can convey no more than an inkling of it, no more than the honeybee can carry on its leg from the full honeycomb. In the first choir is bliss, the greatest of all the gifts they have, in the second choir there is gentleness, in the third there is loveliness; in the fourth sweetness, in the fifth happiness; in the sixth noble fragrance, in the seventh splendor, in the eight dignity; in the ninth ardent love, in the sweet void, pure holiness.

My Journey with Mechthild of Magdeburg

Mechthild has a very quiet nature and she speaks in soft humble tones. You could feel the radiant love for God emanating from every pore of her being as she spoke, always serving you to the best of her ability.

She started praying for the days we are living in, and the souls that needed saving in our era, it was as if her whole desire was for Christianity as a faith, not just one region, tribe or culture, she prayed for the faithful to become more busy with the unsaved, and then prayed for the sinners to become believers, she almost wailed about the state of the global church, yet like a mature old grandmother, she prayed with authority and great faith in what God is able to do in our era.

During this time of prayer, we moved into the throne room and the deeper realities of the throne room of God started to open as she showed me her view of this beautiful place. Rainbows and colors beyond our own capacity of humanity to understand. Inside the depths of this place, the sounds were deafening, if felt like everything, at once wanted to bring praise, and glory to the divine nature of the Creator God. The whole of creation, like a giant symphony of color, sound and just complete light emanations reflected in every angle, and it became completely overwhelming to behold.

I heard her quote the scripture, "God is able to do abundantly more than we can think or imagine".

Some of the prayers she prayed made more sense now, most of the authority and conviction she prayed with, settled into me, I realized, God is not just on the throne, watching creation. Creation is intimately involved in the reality of God, in the nature of who God is, and God is fully invested in the earth, becoming a place where His Glory is shining, expressing and deeply emanating His complete love and majestic power simultaneously.

We understand creation from our viewpoint. When men create something it's always in an inanimate object. Meaning the object that you're creating is not a living object. Man cannot create a living being. Our closest experience of engaging with creating is our children. But even in the process of creating our children, they are still separate from us because we don't create the soul.

We can only create a body in biology, we are only involved in the biological process of procreation. But humanity is not involved in creating a soul, God creates the soul, creates consciousness. God interacts with creation, because God is intimately involved in creation, it's not separate from Him.

God is intimately connected to creation. He has a different understanding of the interplay of creation in His being. Creation is always a place where God expresses himself to men, and to the world, it's the place where God shows who He is.

When humanity is involved in the throne room and when humanity's involved with God. It's not two separate entities. It's almost like this flowing when we God's desire, and man's desire flows into each other, and then start creating something that's new and different and expresses who God is. But what is created inside of men. Is Love, a desire to be united with God.

We are the only beings in the universe that's created in the image and likeness of God. But, in the interplay of the throne room. Creation is not separate from God. God doesn't sit on top of creation and is impersonal personally involved is intrinsically involved. The only reason that creation can be creation is because God is part of creation.

God is the substance that keeps creation created. He's the very essence of the atoms inside creation. That makes creation. That makes it work. The moment he takes himself out of creation ceases to exist because he's the animating principle. God animates creation.

QUESTIONS

1. Which part of her life did you enjoy the most ?

2. From the extracts of her writings which part did you enjoy the most ?

3. Do you think our understanding of creation is changing ?

4. If the big bang is true, is this opposed to the creation of God ?

CHAPTER 9
Jeanne Guyon

"If knowing answers to life's questions is absolutely necessary to you, then forget the journey. You will never make it. For this is a journey of unknowable -- of unanswered questions, enigmas, incomprehensible, and most of all, things unfair."

Jeanne Guyon

Born:	1648
Died:	1717
Nationality:	French
Location:	Geneva | Blois
Outlook:	Catholic
Scribe & Confessor:	Fr. François La Combe
Books:	Life of Madame Guyon, Written by Herself
	Spiritual Opuscules
	Spiritual Torrents
	The Short and Easy Method of Prayer
Interests:	Mystic, writer
Achievements:	Influence on the French Royal court
Key Teachings:	Quite and inner prayer, Grace vs Works

Introduction to Madame Guyon

Madame Guyon was born on 13 April 1648 to a wealthy family in Montargis, south of Paris. Her family neglected her education as they moved 9 times within the period of 10 years. The training she did receive was very religious and based on writings of St Francis de Sales, and other writings by nuns.

She entered an arranged marriage with Jacques Guyon who was a wealthy gentleman from Montargis. There was a substantial age gap between them, she was 15 years old, and he was 38 years old at the time of their wedding.

Her marriage was very unhappy, and she struggled with her maid servant and mother in law. Her half-sister, mother and son all died in the first few years of her marriage, then in 1672 her father and daughter died, this caused her much grief and sorrow.

Her husband died in 1676, after 12 years of marriage, leaving her with three children. She became a widow at 28 years old.

In 1680, after her 3rd mystical experience, she left for Geneva, the local bishop persuaded her to use her wealth to set up a house for "new Catholics" in Gex, with the aim of converting the local protestants.

This venture failed as Madame Guyon disagreed with the nuns charged to lead the house. Bishop Jean d'Arenthon d'Alex, who she met in Geneva, sent Father La Combe to remedy the situation. Here she gave over guardianship of her sons to her mother in law, and took leave of all her possessions, only keeping a monthly annuity for herself.

In January 1685 she moved to Grenoble, in France. She moved to Paris to expound on her mystical ideas, however Louis XIV, did not like these ideas he believed she shared with Molinos, a heretic he condemned.

In January 1688 she was arrested in Paris. After 7 months, and many interrogations by the catholic theologians, she was finally released.

François Fénelon, was one of her biggest supporters. He was an Archbishop that had huge influence in the French court. Upon the suspicion of her ideas, Madame Guyon requested that her works be examined by civil and church judges.

In December 1965 she was again arrested in Paris, and imprisoned at Vincennes, and later at the Bastille. In 1699 she began a retraction of her works, theories, and other efforts, and committed to stop spreading her ideas.

She was in captivity at the Bastille until 21 March 1703, her total captivity lasted 7 years. She then moved to Diocese of Blois, a small village where her son lived. She spent 15 years in seclusion, visited by pilgrims from England and Scotland.

In 1704, her books were published in the Netherlands, and she became an international celebrity, among the English and the Germans. They also visited her in Blois.

She died at the age of 69 in Blois, 9 June 1717, still believing herself to be a devout Catholic.

Theology and Doctrine of Madame Guyon

Herewith a few extracts from her works. There is such richness in her writings that time should be spent to really understand the depth of her relationship with God.

A short method of prayer – Page 7

Prayer is the key of perfection and of sovereign happiness; it is the efficacious means of getting rid of all vices and of acquiring all virtues; for the way to become perfect is to live in the presence of God. He tells us this Himself: "Walk before me and be you perfect" (Gen. xvii. 1). Prayer alone can bring you into His presence and keep you there continually.

A short method of prayer – Page 9

This faith in the presence of God within our hearts must lead us to enter within ourselves, collecting our thoughts, and preventing their wandering; this is an effectual way of getting rid of distracting thoughts, and of losing sight of outward things, in order to draw near to God, who can only be found in the secret place of our hearts, which is the sancta-sanctorum in which He dwells.

A short method of prayer – Page 11

Let us apply this method to the Lord's Prayer. We say "Our Father," thinking that God is within us, and will indeed be our Father. After having pronounced this word Father, we remain a few moments in silence, waiting for this heavenly Father to make known His will to us.

Then we ask this King of Glory to reign within us, abandoning ourselves to Him, that He may do it, and yielding to Him the right that He has over us.

If we feel here an inclination to peace and silence, we should not continue, but remain thus so long as the condition may last; after which we proceed to the second petition,

"Your will be done on earth, as it is in heaven." We then desire that God may accomplish, in us and by us, all His will; we give up to God our heart and our liberty, that He may dispose of them at His pleasure. Then, seeing that the occupation of the will should be love, we desire to love, and we ask God to give us His love. But all this is done quietly, peacefully, and so on with the rest of the prayer.

A short method of prayer – Page 11

When the presence of God is given, and the soul begins to taste of silence and repose, this experimental sense of the presence of God introduces it to the second degree of prayer.

A short method of prayer – Page 12

The second degree has been variously termed Contemplation, The Prayer of Silence, and of repose; while others again have called it the Prayer of Simplicity; and it is of this last term that I shall make use here, being more appropriate than that of Contemplation, which signifies a degree of prayer more advanced than that of which I speak.

A short method of prayer – Page 12, Chapter 3

If it leaves you, excite your will by means of some tender affection, and if you then find that your former state of peace has returned, remain in it. The fire must be blown softly, and as soon as it is lighted, cease to blow it, or you will put it out. It is also necessary that you should go to God, not so much to obtain something from Him, as to please Him, and to do His will; for a servant who only serves his master in proportion to the recompense he receives, is unworthy of any remuneration.

A short method of prayer – Page 24

Hearing is the sense given to enable us to receive the words which are communicated to us. Hearing is rather a passive than an active sense, receiving, and not communicating. Christ being the Word which is to be communicated, the soul must be attentive to this Word which speaks within it.

A short method of prayer – Page 26

We should not seek to do anything for ourselves when God acts more excellently in us and for us. It is hating sin as God hates it to hate it in this way. This love, which is the operation of God in the soul, is the purest of all love. All we have to do then is to remain as we are.

A short method of prayer – Page 28

The soul is no sooner called to inward silence, than it should cease to utter vocal prayers; saying but little at any time, and when it does say them, if it finds any difficulty, or feels itself drawn to silence, it should remain silent, and make no effort to pray, leaving itself to the guidance of the Spirit of God.

A short method of prayer – Page 29

A truly humble soul does not marvel at its weakness, and the more it perceives its wretchedness, the more it abandons itself to God, and seeks to remain near to Him, knowing how deeply it needs His help.

A short method of prayer – Page 29

In distractions or temptations, instead of combating them directly, which would only serve to augment them, and to wean us from God, with whom alone we ought to be occupied, we should simply turn away from them, and draw nearer to God; as a little child, seeing a fierce animal approaching it, would not stay to fight it, nor even to look at it, but would run for shelter to its mother's arms, where it would be safe

A short method of prayer – Page 31

Prayer is the heat of love, which melts and dissolves the soul, and carries it to God. In proportion as it melts, it gives out its odour, and this odour comes from the love which burns it.

Personal Journey with Madame Guyon

While understanding that Madame Guyon is one of the great mystics of her age, the first time I encountered her she said something very simple to me and looking back had a profound impact on my understanding of the work of the mystics.

"Not all saintliness is sinlessness", – and explained our great desire to keep ourselves from any offensive works towards Jesus, is sometimes our greatest obstacle.

Self-righteousness has no place in the life of the believer, if we focus on the work of Jesus, we accept His profound gift of mercy and grace, and then live a life without sin conciseness, our desire to live according to the flesh slowly disappears. As our eyes are simply fixed on Him, this gaze will guide our hearts into the ways of our actions.

On another occasion, while reading some of her work on the simple prayer, Madame Guyon appeared before me and asked me to listen to her explanation of the creation of God, as He showed it to her.

As she opened her revelation of creation, I saw the inner desires of God, as He wanted to create the world, God the Father had an intimate and great longing for revelation of His heart. I saw the deepest desires in the heart of Abba, and only Jesus, the son of God could express or reveal these deep secret things.

When God said let there be light, the word could also be, let there be revealed. Jesus became the only being in creation, able to reveal the inner most hearts desires, colliding with the inner most thoughts of God into a manifestation of creation.

The whole creation was a true reflection, and revelation of the love of God in every aspect. Un-fallen creation was so pure, so holy, and so expressive of the divine, no existent being could deny the beauty and goodness of God.

The moment where the thought of God, and the heart of God, collided, into what some may call the "all spark" or "big bang" – the moment of creation, where these deep desires beyond words, and the deepest thoughts, beyond what we can even say, become an emanation, then a creation, and everything became a universal mirror of the divine goodness, for the first time in eternity, time existed, space existed, because Jesus Christ was slain before the foundation, and created a separation, a veil of creation, where the beauty of God could be revealed in materiality.

Then once Jesus died on the Cross, He once again entered into this pre-foundational place, and tore the veil, this enabled Jesus to become the interface into the uncreated creation, the place where we could not access, where only God could be, and no human could be. Jesus became the glasses for the sons of God to access the divine, the realms beyond the fallen creation, the realms of God, beyond the heavens, beyond everything we know currently.

Every place where Jesus Christ could access, we now have access, we might not be dimensionally mature, or perceptually mature, yet Jesus becomes our perception, our ability to even perceive this place beyond our current time and space dimensionality.

This is not the cosmic Jesus, or the galactic Jesus, In the Holy Place, the veil has been torn, in this place of complete one-ness, this place of union, the multi dimensionality of creation become dimension-less.

In this place, time and space does not exist, eternity and non-locality become a reality. The quantum reality is expanded, and one becomes clearly entangled into the non-materiality of God. In Hebraic thought this is sometimes called Ayin Sof, or just Ayin – the timeless and space-less place, beyond the beyond.

I had read about these ideas, but seeing them in action, and coming into the full reality of these ideas in the spiritual dimension is very hard to explain, and in reality, beyond my ability to explain. I only aim to invite you into these places, as I write, the heavens are open to you, my dear reader.

"Sometimes God is bigger than we think, or believe, outside of ourselves worlds are left to explore" – Madame Guyon

QUESTIONS

1. Which part of her life did you find intriguing ?

2. From the extracts of her writing which part did you enjoy the most ?

3. Do you think our idea of history of the earth and civilization is changing ?

CHAPTER 10
Gertrude the Great

"O Sacred Heart of Jesus, fountain of eternal life, Your Heart is a glowing furnace of Love. You are my refuge and my sanctuary. O my adorable and loving Savior, consume my heart with the burning fire with which Yours is aflame. Pour down on my soul those graces which flow from Your love. Let my heart be united with Yours. Let my will be conformed to Yours in all things. May Your Will be the rule of all my desires and actions. Amen."

Gertrude the Great

Born:	1256
Died:	1302
Nationality:	Italian
Location:	Helfta (Germany)
Outlook:	German Benedictine Nun
Books:	The Herald of God's Loving-Kindness
	Spiritual Exercises
Interests:	Theology
Achievements:	Leader of the monastic community
Key Teachings:	Devotion to the Sacred Heart of Christ, Meditation, Prayer
Canonized:	1677

The Life of Gertrude the Great

Gertrude was born in 1256 in Eisleben, current Germany. At the age of 4 years she entered the school at the monastery of St Mary at Helfta. The monastery abbess was Gertrude of Hakeborn, a well-known mystic in her own right.

In 1281 she started encountering visions, and spiritual experiences, she was 25 at the time. Gertrude was a very gifted student, focusing on secular knowledge, these experiences shifted her interest towards Theology, doctrine and the scriptures. She was well versed in the church fathers like Augustine, and Gregory the Great, as well as her contemporary Bernard of Clairvaux.

Gertrude devoted herself to prayer and meditation and started writing spiritual works for the benefit of her sisters. She was known for her generosity towards others, and doing what came into hear head, others called her a bit impulsive, but she felt it was obedience to the divine will.

Gertrude died at Helfta near Eisleben in 1302.

Theology of Gertrude the Great

One of Gertrude's key theological focuses was "nuptial mysticism", that is, she came to see herself as the bride of Christ. Although this is still something we focus on in current Christianity, her understanding of this nuptial relationship is focused on a covenantal understanding, due to the nuns being celibate.

The nature of this relationship is then the relationship between the beloved, and the bridegroom, as in Song of Songs, this is a metaphorical relationship, focused on spiritual union, and a growth in love and affection for the divine nature of God.

Some of the portions extracted from her work, is more to indicate what I felt would resonate with most of my readers, however I would encourage to read her works, and dig for the diamonds in her writing for yourself.

The intention, as previously stated, is not to explain the theology of each Saint, or give my own view points, but to rather discover they unique journey with God, in their own time, and place, and celebrate the unique voice of God in their time and place.

The Herald of God's loving kindness – Page 101, Chapter 1 of Book 2: How the Lord first visited her as the dayspring from on High

At the hour already mentioned, then I was standing in the middle of the dormitory. In meeting an elder sister, according to the custom of our Order I bowed my head. As I raised it, I saw standing beside me a young man. He was lovely and refined and looked about sixteen; his appearance was such as my youth would find pleasing. With kindly face and gentle words, he said to me, "your salvation will come quickly; why are you consumed by sadness? Do you have no counsellor, that sorrow has overwhelmed you?"

The Herald of God's loving kindness – Page 107, Chapter 3 of Book 2: The pleasantness of the Lords indwelling

For preserving so a great gift I offer you that most excellent prayer which as your bloody sweat testifies, the pain of strait necessity made strong, the innocence of pure simplicity made devout and the love of white-hot divinity made potent. By the power of that same most perfect prayer, perfect me completely in union, with you and draw me to yourself in my heart of hearts. Then whenever it happens that I'm devote myself to external works for practical purposes, may I be given to them on loan.

The Herald of God's loving kindness – Page 113, Chapter 5 of Book 2: The Wound of Love

Suddenly you where there unexpectedly, opening a wound in my heart with these words: "May all your emotions come together in this place; that is may the sum total of your delight, hope, joy, sorrow, fear and your other emotions be fixed firmly in my love".

The Herald of God's loving kindness – Page 125, Chapter 9 of Book 2: The Indissoluble Union of her Soul

O gift that is above every gift, to be satisfied so abundantly in the store-room by the sweet scents of the divine! And in the wine cellar, hutch of pleasure, to become so overflowingly drunk on the wine of love, even to be drowned, so that on is no suffered to take the slightest step toward those distant lands where the power of such fragrance is likely to grow faint!

No only that: as often as it might be necessary to travel there under the guidance of love, what a gift is it is to carry with one the lingering aftertaste of such total satisfaction, that one may be able to offer sweet odors from the divine richness of abundant sweetness.

The Herald of God's loving kindness – Page 128, Chapter 10 of Book 2: The Influence of God

Your usual loving-kindness, my God, gently lightened this burden and refreshed my soul with these words: "Since you found the rushing flood of those torrents of no use, I shall draw you to my divine heart so that I may flow gently and sweetly into you, rhythmically and proportioned to your capacity".

The Herald of God's loving kindness – Page 132, Chapter 12 of Book 2: Bearing with Human Inadequacy

You appeared to me in the form of a vagrant, so that I might judge from your appearance that you were completely forlorn, bereft of possessions and power. Then my conscience, guilty because of it's recent lapse, gnawed at me and lamenting I began to ponder how outrageous it was to be a trouble to you, the source of perfect purity and peace, with the stings of the vices tat disturb me.

<u>My experience with Gertrude the Great</u>

Ah! Gertrude the Great. She is simply great in her thinking, communicating and understanding of our need as a society to belong.

She started our conversation with discipline as this was a grave concern for her. She lamented that our era has lost the value for discipline. She explained how spiritual disciplines like prayer, meditation on the word, and scripture reading, created a place where God could encounter people, without the need for emotional or spiritual experiences, just the reality of the word, encountering Christians.

Her concern was based on the current path of Christianity towards chaos, where the word of God was just another book that could be searched on google, and quickly understood. She explained that most Christians are starting to see discipline as religion, mere actions to please God, instead of understanding the nature of continued focus, and actions to create a platform for understanding and encounter.

The tendency by many in Christianity to call any acts of ritual and sacred practice, religion, would become their grates enemy of mastery.

The spiritual reality of acceleration did not excuse Jesus from going up the mountain to spend time with Father God, if the Son of God has a daily prayer ritual, surly the rest of the faithful Christians might follow the example of the Master.

All of us connect symbols and meaning of symbols to our daily lives. Whether it is a song being played during the day that has special meaning, or the way we enter our house in a certain manner. We remember things through symbols, meanings, sights and sounds.

Why then do we not value these things in our relationship with God? Why do we minimize the existence of truth and symbols hidden in plain sight? Gertrude described the Egyptian system of hieroglyph texts, and the Chinese written pictographs as the current future of language to explain a concept of bringing value into symbols and pictures. She explained that as the consciousness of the earth increases, we will need higher levels of communication due to the speed of the ideas being processed. So, for us as Christians even more, we need to increase our capacity to understand and value symbols, pictures and colours.

We have all felt inadequate at some stage trying to use flat alphabetic language to explain something, our ability to communicate deep spiritual meaning is often very hard.

We walk into churches and cathedrals and just see beautiful pictures, and paintings all over the place, and like the fool, we walk out of these places with many photos, but very little revelation of the symbolic meaning, or the deeper reality behind the symbolic.

A culture that is not able to communicate in metaphors and symbols will never be able to fully comprehend spiritual truth. This will then translate into people that will read the holy scriptures based on face value, losing the spiritual realities beyond.

If we are going to be a faith that changes the nature of the world, we will need to become painters with words and pictures, melted together in sacred symbology, and revealing the beauty of Jesus in carefully thought out symbols, that speak many words in a simple picture.

The language of God is not just sound, or color, images or words, the language of God is truth, manifested by Jesus in person, but communicated to humanity by living letters, moving epistles called Christians, sons and daughters of a Father, that is much more than just words or pictures on a page.

The earth is about to move into pneumatic technology, or atmospheric technology, where ideas and pictures will be communicated using the dimensions of "spiritual world" around us, this will highly elevate the human ability to create, those who dominate the dialogue, will be those who speak in symbols, or dark speech, as some would say.

Gertrude concluded that the symbol becomes the inflection point where beauty and truth meet, to shift the culture into a new dimension of discovery and intellectual maturity.

The harvest in the earth will only increase, if the church and Christianity at large is able to more accurately reflect the beauty and goodness of Jesus, this means the revelation of God in your era, your epoch is about to explode into the brightest moment in history, as many will come to Christ, being exposed to His marvelous light, the divine light of Jesus shining though the Sons, into creation.

When the renaissance happened, the mystics created a spiritual reality by the divine revelation they received, this built a culture where the whole culture could change, the church did not accept most of the ideas, and hence, the reformation happened, due to the inability to integrated this massive change into the dominant culture.

The same situation is about to start from 2020 onwards, as the mystical revelations of the dimensions of the heavens open up, the cultural and intellectual shift will start occurring, the question is, will the leaders of the current structures embrace this new normal, or will they become more irrelevant as technological and scientific development explodes.

What does the gospel sound like to those living on a Mars colony? Can Jesus save people based in space, or do they need to live on earth of serve the God of creation?

"You are living in the greatest moments of history, your generation will develop and see things change on a scale that has not been seen for millennia, I trust you will take hold of the opportunity God is pouring into the earth, to develop ideas that will change the face of the earth, and display the goodness of God." – Gertrude

QUESTIONS

1. Which part of her life did you enjoy

2. Which part of the extracts did you like, is there any part you disagree with ?

3. Do you think our language can evolve into more complexity ?

4. Do you like emoji cons and why ?

5. Has somebody misunderstood your emoji cons, or have they helped you communicate better ?

CHAPTER 11
Catherine of Siena

"Even if all the sins that could possibly be committed were gathered together

in one person, it would be like a drop of vinegar in the sea" [of God's mercy].

Catherine of Siena

Born:	25 March 1347
Died:	29 April 1380 (33)
Nationality:	Italian
Location:	Rome
Outlook:	Dominican Nun
Scribe & Confessor:	Raymond of Capua
Books:	The Dialogue of Divine Providence
	Little Supplement Book (Tommaso d'Antonio Nacci da Siena)
	Life of Catherine (Raymond of Capua)
Interests:	Church politics in Rome
Achievements:	Doctor of the Church
Key Teachings:	Mystical marriage, Stigmata
Supernatural Miracles:	Stigmata
Canonized:	29 June 1461

The Life of Catherine of Sienna

Catherine was born in Sienna in Tuscany, Italy, on 25 March 1347, she was the daughter of a cloth dyer and poet. Her mother had 22 children of which 11 died at birth or early childhood. She was known as a child with great joy, her parents gave her a nick name "Euphrosyne", which means joy.

At the age of 5 she had her first vision of Christ, and at the age of 7 she vowed to give her whole life to God.

One of her sisters died while giving birth and her parents wanted her to marry her brother in law. This she resisted vehemently by fasting and cutting her long beautiful hair. She resisted the convent and the marriage bed, and kept her Dominican way, her parents relented eventually.

She received the habit of the Dominican tertiary from the friars, initially the tertiary "nuns" objected since they were only widows in the order until this time. Catherine remained at home, however she lived in silence and solitude, keeping to the Dominican traditions.

Catherine at the age of 21 received visions of being married to Jesus, or her "mystical marriage to Jesus", there was some controversy regarding this experience, but the result was Jesus asking her to join public life and serve the poor and needy in society.

She made her first journey to Florence in 1374 to be interviewed by the Dominican authorities, they accepted her testimony. In 1375 she went to Pisa to persuade the political leaders towards loyalty for the pope.

In 1376, she went to Avignon as ambassador of the Republic of Florence, to make peace with the Papal states. She failed at this attempt, but the city of Florence later succeeded due to her efforts.

In 1377 she returned to Sienna and founded her women's monastery, she also had some spiritual experiences at this time, and started writing her work, "Dialogues", at this time.

Catherine trained herself in extreme fasting, and her friends and tutors all admonished her to eat properly. In 1380 she lost the use of her legs, and later that year she suffered a stroke, and died in Rome on 29 April 1380.

Her last words were, *"Father, into Your Hands I commend my soul and my spirit."*

Theology and revealed truth of St Catherine of Sienna

The life of this remarkable women has been marked with suffering and loss. She lost her mother and close relatives at an early age, the few remaining friends, and adopted family left her for the call to become nuns in the church, limiting her access to them.

Her plea to enter the enclosed order of nuns to the Pope of her time, opened the possibility for her to become the youngest nun to be accepted, and the youngest doctor of the church. Paul admonishes Timothy, "don't allow others to treat you according to your age", this lesson seems to be one of the first replicated in her life.

This determination and perseverance served her well as she faced the discipline and focus of monastic life, and her focus on the call of God, and the discipline of prayer.

Dialogue of St Catherine – Page 25

This knowledge of yourself and of Me is found in the earth of true humility, which is as wide as the diameter of the circle, that is as the knowledge of self and of Me (for, otherwise, the circle would not be without end and beginning, but would have its beginning in knowledge of self, and its end in confusion, if this knowledge were not contained in Me). Then the tree of love feeds itself on humility, bringing forth from its side the off-shoot of true discretion, in the way that I have already told you, from the heart of the tree, that is the affection of love which is in the soul, and the patience, which proves that I am in the soul and the soul in Me. This tree then, so sweetly planted, produces fragrant blossoms of virtue, with many scents of great variety, inasmuch as the soul renders fruit of grace and of utility to her neighbor, according to the zeal of those who come to receive fruit from My servants; and to Me she renders the sweet odor of glory and praise to My Name, and so fulfills the object of her creation.

"In this way, therefore, she reaches the term of her being, that is Myself, her God, who am Eternal Life. And these fruits cannot be taken from her without her will, inasmuch as they are all flavored with discretion, because they are all united, as has been said above."

Jesus as the Bridge for Humanity, St Catherine – Page 33

Wherefore I have told you that I have made a Bridge of My Word, of My only-begotten Son, and this is the truth. I wish that you, My children, should know that the road was broken by the sin and disobedience of Adam, in such a way, that no one could arrive at Eternal Life. Wherefore men did not render Me glory in the way in which they ought to have, as they did not participate in that Good for which I had created them, and My truth was not fulfilled. This truth is that I have created man to My own image and similitude, in order that he might have Eternal Life, and might partake of Me, and taste My supreme and eternal sweetness and goodness.

Dialogue of St Catherine – Page 67

WHEN the soul has passed through the doctrine of Christ crucified, with true love of virtue and hatred of vice, and has arrived at the house of self-knowledge and entered therein, she remains, with her door barred, in watching and constant prayer, separated entirely from the consolations of the world.

Dialogue of St Catherine – Page 75

You see then that the saints and every soul in Eternal Life have desire for the salvation of souls without pain, because pain ended in their death, but not so the affection of love.

Thus, as if drunk with the Blood of the Immaculate Lamb, and clothed in the love of the neighbor, they pass through the Narrow Gate, bathed in the Blood of Christ crucified, and they find themselves in Me, the Sea Pacific, raised from imperfection, far from satiety, and arrived at perfection, satisfied by every good.

The Small Door of Obedience, Dialogue of St Catherine – Page 124

Such as these have undertaken to open the little door, doing without the great key of general obedience, which opens the door of Heaven, as I have said to you. They have taken a little key, passing through a low and narrow opening in the great door. This small door is part of the great door, as you may see in any real door. They should keep this key when they have got it, and not throw it away. And because the truly obedient have seen with the light of faith that they will never be able to pass through this little door with the load of their riches and the weight of their own will without great fatigue and without losing their life, and that they cannot walk with head erect without breaking their neck;

Reward for those who Labor, Dialogue of St Catherine – Page 131

I have appointed you all to labor in the vineyard of obedience in different ways, and every man will receive a price, according to the measure of his love, and not according to the work he does, or the length of time for which he works, that is to say, that he who comes early will not have more than he who comes late, as My Truth told you in the holy gospel by the example of those who were standing idle and were sent by the lord of the vineyard to labor; for he gave as much to those who went at dawn.

Powers of the Soul, Dialogue of St Catherine – Page 133

I also showed you, to give you further light concerning My truth, how this Bridge is built on three steps; that is, on the three powers of the soul. These three steps I also represented to you, as you know, under figures of your body -- the feet, the side, and the mouth -- by which I also figured three states of soul -- the imperfect state, the perfect state, and the most perfect state, in which the soul arrives at the excellence of unitive love. I have shown you clearly in each state the means of cutting away imperfection and reaching perfection, and how the soul may know by which road she is walking and of the hidden delusions of the devil and of spiritual self-love.

Personal experience of St Catherine of Sienna

A meeting with St Catherine felt more like a stately visit, than having tea with your favorite friend. She has a measured tone to her voice, and every action she does is thought out, nothing just happens around this lady.

She was seated in a dimension of God related to a specific place in His heart for maturing of the sons, and her whole understanding and focus was the history of humanity, and the understanding that we have a role to play in history.

The culture of honor and humility in heaven demands a response of maturity. How you respond to those with virtue in heaven, mirror the maturity of the person being the focus of God in that moment of time.

All of heaven is invested in the sons of God coming into maturity, and focusing on the values of heaven, not just the actions, but the underlying motivations, the intentions and the ideas behind the spiritual metaphor, and the places of encounter.

John mentioned in the bible: "I see a new heaven, and a new earth coming" – this means the heavens we are accessing now, will be different once Jesus comes to earth for a second time, even the very throne room of God will change, based on the maturing of the sons to take responsibility to govern places in the kingdom.

This may sound strange to some but does the bible not say; "I will give you 10 cities if you were faithful on earth?" If God is going to give us cities, we will need to learn how the culture and value system of heaven operates, so that the cities we ultimately govern, starts holding the pattern of the one Above, Jesus the Author.

Another scripture "The pattern of the Jerusalem above, the Jerusalem below"; What is this divine pattern then, how shall we start learning this new way of living, - by living in the way of Love?

I asked about why some of these truths were not revealed directly in her book, Catherine showed me a flower in the heavenly dimension.

The flowed slowly started unfurling, like a slow motion movie, one could see the petals slowly unravel, the circles of light inside the flower started expanding, the realms of beauty and the places of spiritual colors started flowing from the flower, like water colors into the air.

She explained further that the appointed time of God then brings this beauty into manifestation on the earth.

Just like small children don't always appreciate complex pieces of beauty like art or sculpture, the acquired taste of beauty is needed to understand the revealing of God in every era in history.

When the bible says, "Taste and see that the Lord is Good", - this is an ever-increasing dimension of beauty being unveiled to the sons of salvation. Like ever growing children, we behold His eternal beauty, and it then increases in complexity and magnitude. Imagine a 4 year old child, and an 80 year old grandfather, looking at an artwork by Rembrandt van Rijn, the child sees only color and believes it to be beautiful, the grandfather, being an artist himself, sees the strokes of the master, holding the paintbrush, and the skill of the colors being mixed to form a very realistic painting.

Heavenly culture unveils the beauty as an ever-increasing revelation of God. The beauty of a restored relationship or economic system or nation is the culture of Christianity effecting political structures on earth.

Catherine explained the coming age of the church, where Christians would again be allowed to speak to the leaders of nations, need to understand not just physical protocols, but also spiritual protocols of rulers.

Her concern for the Christianity of the next era was their lack of understanding of governmental systems, and how the earth is about to move into major upheaval, and change. Change can only be navigated if all the parties involved don't force everybody to just listen to their voice, and hear their views, but build a society where creative ideas are debated in a safe environment, where people don't clamor for recognition, but endeavor towards an outcome.

She explained the need for power to build structures of authority, and how the authority of the believer can never circumvent the structures of understanding in a nation. The eco system of specific regions are based on the spiritual and political dynamics in an area, this cannot be changed by mere hard labour, both spiritual or physical, but the complex interdependence of the system needs to be changed by understanding how to dilute a specific power base, and then to create other structures of power.

These efforts to diversify the power structures will need to managed by people of honour, and building a culture where all the voices in the room have power, have input, and can make decisions for the group, without diluting the capacity of the group, or the potent power of the leaders.

Negotiating and navigating change by looking at power sharing initiatives cannot be the sole solution. The ministry of reconciliation which Christ gave the church as a body, is about to become a major player in the solving of global political issues, if Christians don't learn how to listen to the Spirit of Wisdom, and bring to bear the divine solutions of God, the disparity of our nations will just result in more conflict, and less resolutions.

QUESTIONS

1. Which part of her life resonates with you ?

2. Which of the extracts do you disagree with ?

3. Do you believe the face of the church has changed in the past 10 years ?

4. Do you think the church still has a voice in society ?

5. Does government and political leaders care what the church says ?

6. How do you think we can make the voice of Christianity louder ?

CHAPTER 12
Saint Brigid of Kildare

"I should like a great lake of ale, for the King of Kings. I should like the family of heaven to be drinking it through time eternal.

You are My Mother, the Mother of Mercy, and the consolation of the souls in Purgatory. O Jesus!"

Brigit of Kildare

Born:	451
Died:	525
Nationality:	Ireland
Location:	Kildare
Outlook:	Celtic Catholic mystic
Co-Abbot :	Conleth
Interests:	Monastic way
Achievements:	Successful monastic communities founded by her in Ireland
Key Teachings:	Practical work fused with Spiritual prayer
Supernatural Miracles:	Turning water into beer, weather miracles, many healings

The Life of Saint Brigid

The details of the life of Bridget seems to be lost in time as she lived a very long time ago. Some contend that Brigid is linked to a goddess of Ireland, with many historians discussing the nature of her life, and the legends of her life, being so close to the same stories being told about the pre-existing goddess of Ireland.

Personally, I don't share these views, hence the inclusion about her life, her influence on Christianity, the church, and the history of the church in the UK. Most of the information I write here, was found in Bede's "Ecclesiastical history of the Church of England".

She was born in 451 AD in Faughart, north of Dundalk, Ireland, her mother was a Christian Pict slave named Brocca, baptized by St Patrick and her father was Dubhthach, a chieftain from Leinster.

Brigid was sold to a druid at birth by her parents, it seems she had a very tough childhood, with many legends and stories of her supernatural survival.

She then took the veil at Mag Tulach, by Saint Mel of Ardagh, in 468 she joined Bishop Mac Caile, to join Saint Mel at the Kingdom of Tethbae.

Brigid started her own monastery at Kildare on 480 called the "Church of the Oak". The monastery was started on the pagan holy site, where a group of young women followed the old ways.

Brigid then invited Conleth, a hermit from Old Connell to help her pastor the subsequent two monastic communities she founded.

She founded a school of art, with subjects like metalwork and illumination. Kildare had a scriptorium which created books and illustrated great works for scholarly endeavors. The Book of Armagh also mentions that Brigid had a friendship with St Patrick, and how they both changed the face of Ireland by serving Christ and performing many miracles.

Brigid died being attended to by Saint Ninnidh, on the 1st of Feburary 525 in Kildare.

Theology of Saint Brigid

Due to the nature of her time, we don't have any surviving documents she wrote, most of her life story was written by others, they hardly tell of her words, yet speak of her life, her actions and the many legends of her life.

Her spirituality is a practical walk, like most of the Celtic saints, her life is known for its practical wisdom, and the situations she was able to deal with. A wisdom from above seems to permeate her life. I will quote some of the legends told about her, believing them to be true, and allowing the reader to glean from her life, the eternal wisdom of Christ, displayed in her actions.

"Another such story tells us that Brigid attended a very sick woman who told her she needed to drink milk or else she would die. Brigid instructed her assistant to bring her a cup of water and to conceal it. She then proceeded to bless the cup after which it was revealed and found to contain milk. The woman drank of the milk and was instantly cured."

"One of the more commonly told stories is of Brigid asking the King of Leinster for land. She told the king that the place where she stood was the perfect spot for a convent. It was beside a forest where the members could collect firewood and berries, there was a lake nearby that would provide water and the land was fertile. The king laughed at her and refused to give her any land. Brigid prayed and asked God to soften the king's heart. Then she smiled at the king and said, "Will you give me as much land as my cloak will cover?" The king thought that she was joking and agreed. She told four of her sisters to take up the cloak, but instead of laying it flat on the turf, each sister, with face turned to a different point of the compass, began to run swiftly, the cloth growing in all directions. The cloak began to cover many acres of land. "Oh, Brigid!" said the frightened king, "what are you about?" "I am, or rather my cloak is about covering your whole province to punish you for your stinginess to the poor." "Call your maidens back. I will give you a decent plot of ground." The saint was persuaded, and if the king held his purse-strings tight in future, she had only to allude to her cloak to bring him to reason. Soon afterwards, the king became a Christian, began to help the poor and commissioned the building of the convent."

"After Brigid promised God a life of chastity, her brothers were annoyed at the loss of a bride price. When she was outside carrying a load past a group of poor people, some began to laugh at her. A man named Bacene said to her, "The beautiful eye which is in your head will be betrothed to a man though you like it or not." In response, Brigid thrust her finger in her eye and said, "Here is that beautiful eye for you. I deem it unlikely that anyone will ask you for a blind girl." Her brothers tried to save her and wash away the blood from her wound, but there was no water to be found. Brigid said to them,

"Put my staff about this sod in front of you", and after they did, a stream came forth from the ground. Then she said to Bacene, "Soon your two eyes will burst in your head", and it happened as she said"

"In one story, Brigid protected a woman from a nobleman who had entrusted a silver brooch to the woman for safekeeping but then secretly had thrown it into the sea. He charged her with stealing it, knowing that he could take her as a slave if a judge ruled in his favour. The woman fled and sought refuge with Brigid's community. By chance, one of her fishermen hauled in a fish which, when cut open, proved to have swallowed the brooch. The nobleman freed the woman, confessed his sin, and bowed in submission to Brigid.[14] A similar story is told of Saint Mungo."

"Brigid's foundations were very successful, and quite prosperous. All the bishops of Ireland wanted her to found convents in their districts.

Brigid once requested of Aillill, a Leinster chieftain, some wattles for building a settlement at Kildare. Aillill had pre- pared the wattles (poles used for laying a thatch roof) for his own houe and refused Brigid's request. Suddenly all the horses fell to the ground and nothing would induce them to get up again. In the end he left the wattles for Brigid.

The Kildare foundation rapidly grew to such magnitude that it became as large as a city and a bishop had to be appointed to the territory". Celtic Flames – Cathy Walters

"Brigid loves music and one time at a chieftain's fortress, somewhere near Knockaney (County Limerick), Brigid went to ask for the release of a captive. She was asked to sit and wait for the chieftain by the man's aged foster-father. While she was waiting, she saw some harps hanging on the wall. She asked for some music but the harpists were not there. The sisters with Brigid told the foster-father to take the harp, and while Brigid was present he would be able to play. The old man took down the harp from the wall, thrummed it clumsily, but suddenly found he could produce airs and harmonies. Another of the household anxiously tried a second harp with the same results.

Presently the place was filled with happy music and the chieftain arrived home to hear it. He heard rare laughter from his foster-father. Pleased with his homecoming he con- ceded to Brigid all that she asked". Celtic Flames – Cathy Walters

"Another time Brigid saw a man passing by her gates car- rying a sack on his back. "What are you carrying?" she asked, knowing that it was much needed salt.

"Stones," said the man who did not want to give up any of his salt.

"Stones? Let it be," she replied. The man's knees began to buckle under a new weight. He stumbled back to Brigid whose word he now feared.

"What have you in that sack?" she asked again.

"Salt." He replied.

"Let it be," said Brigid. And immediately it was salt". **Celtic Flames – Cathy Walters**

My Experience with Saint Brigid

As I read the works of Bridget I was inspired by her life. During this time, I encountered her, such an honour to be able to interact with her. I was fascinated by her life and knowing all the miracles and signs and wonders she performed on earth, I asked Bridget what keys she could give me for the manifestation of heaven, and the release of these miracles in our era.

Her answer to the question was very unexpected: *"Kevin, you want to create moments for miracles in very small timeframes, and with a very set way to think about miracles. Your ideas of what miracles are, links very much to your Pentecostal way of thinking, you want to do what Jesus did, the way He did it so people can accept the wonders you perform".*

"Signs are designed to offend the mind, boggle the natural carnal heart, and tussle with the thought process of this world. I used simple principles of Jesus, the wine into water, I turned water into beer, yet you would think your wine more holy than my beer, simply because the Savior instituted the Passover meal with wine, this was after He turned the water into wine, the culture of His time, was just as offended by the wine as any other miracles they did".

She looked at me in earnest; *"Your day will be filled with many signs that make people wonder, many miracles that offend the minds of the carnal man, the question is will you follow the signs to their divine path, or will you write books about the signs, and become even more famous for the stories, and less famous for the word of the Lord in the moment".*

"Signs point to something, they always speak beyond the immediate moment, into the eternal now, the eternal divine intention. Your generation should get ready for signs that are really offensive, and very controversial, look for the extra ordinary, look for the weird and wonderful fingertips of God in the mundane moments of life, and realize, if you are grateful for the small miracles in your everyday life, and you celebrate every small moment,

the moments of time will increase, and in these pockets of time, miracles manifest without effort, without all the hard work you currently want to do, to "make" things happen".

"The divine order of miracles is based on the cup of suffering intersecting with the cup of provision, pouring divine mercy into the current timeline of your reality".

Suddenly the scenery in the realm we were in changed, nature seemed to flow into the place we were speaking, and the colors of nature flowed like rivers into this very small space, if felt like there was not enough space for the beauty of creation to enter this small realm I was sitting in with her.

"I want to talk to you about restoring of nature Kevin", I looked at her, and wondered why this topic now. *"You should know the Father loves to speak to His sons about nature, it was His original task to Adam, "Tend the Garden", and the Father expects you to also do what the first Adam could not complete".*

"A misunderstanding of nature is an abuse of the nature of God, your epoch is entering into a more focused conservation of nature, as you start taking better practical care of nature, the very nature of God will be revealed in a deeper way".

"God the Father will not reveal more of Himself to stewards who are not willing to lay down their lives for the place of stewardship they have received. How will God reveal more of Himself to this generation, by allowing themselves to show themselves "faithful in the little", and in this case, some of this assignment will be nature itself. The reason your culture has abused creation, is your worship of reason, intellectualism and your selfish ambition to become independent from God, has created the situation where the created creature man, wants to show He was not ultimately created, but existed independently. The most destructive child is the child who believes he is completely independent and living isolated from his surroundings".

"In this next phase of humanity's maturing process, God the Father will once again reveal His divine magnificent heart of love, His love will bring the orphan to repentance, and the destroyer will be silenced by love again. The release of global interconnected thinking, and quantum theories, that support the existence of this quantum entangled world will cause your generation to see not just the global eco system as connected, but to understand the spiritual eco system of interconnected faith-based systems".

"Jesus created one Body, the global body of Christ, this body exists outside of space and time, this body is linked like an eco-system, and this earthly time

based body of Christianity will now start to become merged with the global eternal body of believers, the church of the first born".

"As we all link hands over the seasons of the earth, and the epoch of time, the global eternal church, will become the maturing sons, that tend the earth, and multiply, the end will once again reflect the beginning".

"The tree of life, Jesus crucified on the earth, now bringing the fruits of the nations to the table of Abba Father, declaring the goodness of God to all the galaxies of creation, the multiverses, to say humanity is the crown of God's creation, redeemed by the one and only Redeemer".

Bridget came to encourage and challenge the mindset of her time, and even now I feel we are challenged to change the way we perceive signs, wonders, miracles and nature. A challenge to dare believe that we to can make a difference if we focus on Christ.

QUESTIONS

1. Which part of her Celtic story did you like ?

2. From the stories about her miracles, which one did you like ?

3. Does Celtic spirituality still have something to say regarding nature in our society ?

4. Should we believe in signs and wonders ?

5. Why does God use signs and wonders ?

BONUS *Chapter*

BONUS CHAPTER
Kristos Samra

(Krəstos Śämra)

Born:	1500 AD
Died:	Unknown
Nationality:	Ethiopian
Location:	Gʷangʷət (Ethiopia)
Outlook:	Ethiopian Orthodox church
Scribe & Confessor:	Filəp̈p̈os (Phillip)
Books:	hagiography (Life Story)
Interests:	Prayer, Solitude
Achievements:	One of only 8 women in Ethiopia who has a haplography written about her.
Key Teachings:	Mercy and Peace of God
Supernatural miracles:	Dead raisings, healings

Introduction and Historical context of Ethiopian Christian Culture

Christianity started in Ethiopia in the 4[AD], which makes the church one of the oldest churches in the history of Christianity, they developed a monastic system with scriptoriums to study the bible and other ancient texts.

The Ethiopians sent delegations to Europe in the 1400s, and they had a strong impact in the Council of Florence (1431-49).

The Portuguese sent Christopher da Gama with Portuguese troops in the mid-1500s to help protect the country against the Islamic invasions.

The emperor Zara Yaeqob ruled for 35 years from 1434 to 1469, he was the major figure in the society, and focused on reforming the church, and focusing Ethiopian affections for the virgin Mary.

The Life of Kristos Samra

The autobiography of Kristos Samra was written in Geez and has been translated to Italian, however the original work was written by Filepos, who wrote her life story based on her dictation.

She was a fierce strong African lady, born into a noble wealthy African family. Kristos was married to the son of the Emperors priest, (Priests can marry in the Ethiopian Church). The emperor treated her as a daughter, and she had 9 sons and 2 daughters from her marriage to the royal priest's son.

One day in a fit of rage, she killed her servant by putting a firebrand down her throat. This brought her life to a turning point and she promised God to devote her life Him, if God raised her dead servant to life. God raised her servant from the dead and shortly after that she left for Däbrä Libanos – a monastic community in Ethiopia.

A common practice by Ethiopian monastics is to spend time praying in the water. Standing upright, Kristos spent 12 years praying for several hours daily at the monastery in this manner.

Kristos stayed in solitude in monasteries around the lake area Narga Səllase and Ṭana Qirqos. At this time, she had many visions, spoke to Angels and to Jesus about spiritual truths.

The biblical patriarchs also visited her in visions and instructed her to move to Gwangut, also on Lake Ṭana, where she founded her first monastery. She found living with others a huge sacrifice as most monastics of her era including her preferred the life of solitude living as a hermit.

She spent 3 years standing in a pit praying, and another 3 years standing in lake Tana praying for the sisters under her care. Fileṗṗos, one of her monks wrote down her 30 visions and her autobiography.

Kritos Samra was buried at Gwangut, Ethiopia, where her monastery still exists today.

Anecdote about Satan in Gädlä Krəstos Šamra

(English translation by Michael Kleiner and Wendy Laura Belcher)

"So, Christ replied, "Please tell me your heart's desire, my dear Kristos Samra, that which is in your heart."

At that point I replied to him as follows, "My lord, I would like you to pardon the devil, and for all humanity to be saved from being condemned to eternal suffering. Truly, you don't desire the sinner's death, but rather his turning back from sin! This is why I say to you: 'Pardon the devil!' Don't think that I like to say all these things to you. Rather, I do it for the sake of Adam and his offspring, because their flesh is my flesh."

After I had said these things to Christ, our Lord replied with a laugh, "You're asking me for a difficult thing, my dear Kristos Samra! Many saints who were before you have not asked me for this." [p. 46]"

"After saying this, Christ summoned Saint Michael, the head of the angels. He said to him, "Go and take her to Sheol, because she has asked me to liberate the devil from the [realm of] punishment with eternal suffering."

Immediately, Saint Michael, the head of the angels, took me with him to Sheol."

"So I called out for him, in the language of the angels, "Satan!"

Instantly, Satan shouted back, in a loud voice, "Who calls out for me, in the place where I am Lord God of many hosts?"

After Satan had said this, he came to me and told me, "I 've been looking for you for a long time. Today you have finally come to my home."

At this point, I replied to him, "Come out quickly! Our Lord has pardoned you, as well as those who are yours."

When I said this to him, he became enraged.

He seized my left hand and dragged me down to the lowest level of She'ol. However, Saint Michael came to my aid, following me with his sword of fire in his hands. With it,he then struck that bominable creature who knows no mercy."

My experience with Kristos Samra

I would like to start this last chapter by saying that I visited the Ethiopian Orthodox church of Pretoria South-Africa to understand the culture better before even attempting to write anything about this saint. The practices of the church brought such revelation and I am humbled that they afforded me the opportunity to spend that time with them.

I believe that one cannot, and should not write about the saints, unless you have at least made some effort to go to the places where they lived, and experience some of the land they called their home.

Many people write about the African context of Christianity, yet never put their feet into the land of our blessed continent.

The same situation also applies to writing about the saints from other parts of the Christian faith, it's easy to condemn a certain group of Christians who do not share your own doctrine, however once you share bread at their table, and hear about their life, their love for Jesus, and how they tell other faiths about the goodness of Jesus, this judgmental attitude seems very hard to keep maintaining in our hearts.

While attending a service one morning, I experienced Saint Kristos once again, while looking at the worshipers I realized many of them had no personal experience with Jesus, this was just their normal Sunday, the same why that many Christians spend their Sundays.

In this moment she stated that religious people need a religious system. She explained she was concern that I was doing all the right things in this church, yet I had lost the true intention or symbolism. Her correction was towards me, not the situation, bur more the way my heart was situated in the circumstance.

This accounts for Christians as much as it does for any other system in the world, we develop outward works and actions to please God, and then do these actions in the hope of achieving salvation.

This is not the system Jesus gave us; however, Jesus did not bring a culture either, the Jews wanted Jesus to make their culture the world dominant culture. The Hebrew culture although a shadow of Jesus, was not the aim of His coming to earth, God gave the Law, to Moses, this created a culture, although many elements of Jewish culture is divinely inspired, and designed to foreshadow the Christ child, this was not the aim of Jesus.

When Paul writes that there is neither Jew nor Gentile, slave nor free man, male nor female, he is busy removing all the divisions in humanity for the sake of the Good news.

Jesus did not come to bring a heavenly culture, He came to preach the kingdom, to declare a new Era in humanity was at hand, this would be known as the Kingdom of God, and He, Jesus, was the first son of many sons, to bring this new kingdom to earth, and establish the rule of God.

When I understood this, I realized the error of my own ideas, I came to the Ethiopian church, seeking something, trying to find in their culture, and their rules, and in their system some of the hidden gems of Christianity.

While in this culture, I realized that the danger in any church, or denomination, once we start building systems of relationship, the cart is again put in front of the proverbial horse, and yet again, we are building our own way, not the way of Jesus.

The mystery of Jesus, is the relationship He constantly tries to invite us into, Jesus always turns our ideas upside down, " If you want to be first, you need to be last in the kingdom", and other controversial God ideas.

The way of the mystic I realized in this journey, is not the way towards a system of ideas, or a system of hidden revelation, the way of the mystic is more simple, and harder than most roads humanity wants to walk, this way is low, slow, lonely and less traveled than most.

It's the way of the servant, serving all, and yet serving Him, Jesus, the one who served the 12 disciples on His knees, washing their feet, yet realizing this is the moment they have all been waiting for, a moment with the King.

QUESTIONS

1. Which part of the Ethiopian story did you like ?

2. Do you think other denominations in Christianity can teach us something?

3. When you say somebody is religious what do you mean ?

4. What does " kingdom culture " mean ?

5. Does God measure our Good works when we die and reward us based on them ?

MYSTICAL MOTHERS WORTH READING

1. Elisabeth of Schonau

2. Gemma Galgani

3. Marie of the Incarnation

4. Angela of Foligno

5. Margery Kempe

6. Beatrice of Nazareth

7. Elizabeth of the Trinity

8. Hadewijch of Antwerp

9. Maria Faustina Kowalska

10. Caryll Houselander

11. Evelyn Underhill

12. Saint Edith Stein

13. Saint Theresa of Calcutta

14. Marguerite Porete

15. Simone Weil

16. Saint Claire of Assisi

17. Joan of Arc

18. Saint Beatrice of Silva

19. Xenia of st. Petersburg

BIBLIOGRAPHY

1) The collected works of Julian of Norwich published by Revelation-Insight 2009

   ISBN # 978-0-984-1731-5-0

2) Medieval women mystics | Elizabeth Ruth Obbard by New City Press 2002/2007

   ISBN # 978-1-56548-278-4

3) Apparitions of Modern Saints | Patricia Treece by Servant Publications 2001

   ISBN # 1-596-55-303-3

4) The Herald of God's loving-Kindness| Alexandra Barrat by Cistercian Publications 1991

   ISBN # 88679074558

5) Fire in the Spirit | Valarie Tupling Ansdell by FriesenPress 2017

   ISBN # 978-1-4602-9840-4

6) Hilda of Whitby | Ray Simpson by The Bible reading fellowship 2014

7) The Edge of Glory prayers in the Celtic tradition | David Adam by Triangle 1985

   ISBN # 0-281-04197-0

8) Selections from : The flowing Light of the Godhead | Elizabeth A. Anderson by D S Brewer 2003

   ISBN # 978-0-85991-786-5

9) Incandescence | Carmen Acevedo Butcher by Paraclete Press 1993

   ISBN # 1-55725-418-4

10) Interior Castle | E Allison Peers by Random house 1961

    ISBN # 978-0-385-03643-6

11) The complete Madam Guyon| Rev Nancy C James PhD by Paraclete Press 2011

    ISBN # 978-1-55725-923-3

12) Christian Mystics | Carl Macolman by Hampton Roads Publishing company 2016

    ISBN # 978-1-57174-730-3

13) Celtic Flames | Cathy Walters by Good news fellowship ministries, 1999

    ISBN # 1-888081-55-4

TRANSLATIONS

1) Bridget of Sweden- Prophecies and revelations of Saint Bridget of Sweden - www.saintsbooks.net

2) Catharine of Siena – Dialogue of the Seraphic Virgin of Catharine of Siena , Translated by : Algar Thorold , Originally published in 1907 by Kegan Paul, Trench, Trubner & Co., Ltd., London. (Public Domain)

3) Gertrude the great – Herald of God's loving kindness Book 4 Translated by Alexandra Barratt – Liturgical Press, Cistercian Publications, ISBN 9780879075859 (ebook) | ISBN 9780879072858

4) Hildergard of Bingen – Hildergard of bingen selected writings Translated by Mark Atherton – Penguin Books

5) Julian of Norwich- Revelations of Divine love – Translated by Grace Warrack – Published 1901

6) Kristos Samra – The life and Visions of Kristos Samra, a fifteenth century Ethiopian Woman Translations by Michael Klein | Wendy Laura Belcher

7) Madam Jeanne Guyon – A short method of Prayer translated by A.W. Marston, Printed by Ballantyne   and company, Edinburg and London

8) Mechthild of Magdeburg – The flowing light of the Godhead – Translated by Frank Tobin – Published 1997, Paulist Press, ISBN # 9780809137763

9) Saint Brigid – Bede's Ecclesiastical history of England – Translation A.M Sella

10) Cathrine of Genoa – The life and doctrine of Saint Catherine of Genoa – Christian press association publishing CO. 1907

11) St Hilde of Whitby – Bede's Ecclesiastical history of the English nation (c.731) – IV 23-4 , Hilda of Whitby – A spirituality for now – Ray Simpson – The bible reading fellowship – 2014

12) Therese of Lisieux – Autobiography of Saint Theresa of Lisieux – The story of the springtime of a little white flower – first printed in 1922 (Public domain)

13) Saint Theresa of Avila – The way of perfection – E Allison Peers – Image books edition, 1964 ISBN 0-385-06539-6 (Public domain) The interior Castle – Translated by Zimmerman, Benedict , Christian Classics Ethereal Library 1921 (Public Domain) – Transcriber – John Bruno Hare

IMAGE CREDITS:

All images used are from Wikimedia Commons.
Author and CC license stated where available.
https://commons.wikimedia.org/

Julian of Norwich
Rogier van der Weyden / Public domain

Hilda of Whitby
Unknown author / Public domain

Therese of Lisieux
Adrian Michael / Public domain

Teresa of Avila
Peter Paul Rubens / Public domain

Bridget of Sweden
Hermann Rode / Public domain

Saint Catherine of Genoa
Master of Frankfurt / Public domain

Hildegard of Bingen
Unknown author / Public domain

Mechthild of Magdeburg
Robinet Testard / Public domain

Jeanne Guyon
Frankreich. Stahlstich. / Public domain

Gertrude the great
Miguel Cabrera / Public domain

Catherine of Siena
Rutilio di Lorenzo Manetti / Public domain

Saint Brigid of Kildare
Patrick Joseph Tuohy / Public domain

Kristos Samra
Surafel getachew / CC BY-SA
File:Kidist-kirstos-semera.jpg. (2017, April 1). Wikimedia Commons, the
free media repository. Retrieved 08:33, April 21, 2020
from https://commons.wikimedia.org/w/index.php?title=File:Kidist-kirstos-
semera.jpg&oldid=239377154.

ABOUT THE AUTHOR

Kevin Hall is an author, pastor, businessman and father. He loves the local church and to see God move in the nations, he is passionate about Africa, and enjoys special moments with his two boys growing up in South Africa.

Kevin ministers to people searching for the truth of the Gospel, bringing the focus back to the foundations of the Gospel of Jesus Christ.

Kevin founded various ministries during the past few years and successfully handed those ministries over to continue the work that they have started. He is also the CEO of Savantage, an international events and consulting company.

Kevin's heart is to bring people into the fullness of what Father has intended them to be. Bringing people into the understanding that a personal vibrant interactive relationship with Jesus is possible.

Notes

Printed in Great Britain
by Amazon